CLIENT PROFIT SECRETS...

THE PSYCHOLOGICAL
APPROACH
to
SELL REAL ESTATE

7 Strategies to Sell Your Home for an
Additional $30,000 by Marketing like
the Innovator Steve Jobs

IMPACT
MARYLAND REAL ESTATE

with Eric Verdi

i

The *Psychological* Approach to

Sell Real Estate

A Practical Guide to

Increase Your Home's Profit by $30,000

THE *PSYCHOLOGICAL* APPROACH TO SELL REAL ESTATE
7 Strategies to Sell Your Home for an Additional $30,000
by Marketing Like the Innovator Steve Jobs

Steve Jobs affected not one but three industries with his vision and marketing expertise. If the strategies in this book are followed correctly, you'll be able to put an additional $20,000; $30,000; or even $40,000 profit in your pocket when selling your home, and will accomplish what I desire—**A Superior Approach to Positioning your Home for Maximum Profit.**

I have found that most real estate agents have a system, but no strategies to selling homes. A systemic approach is inferior because no two homes should be presented or marketed the same. A strategy, on the other hand, is a set of fundamental principles for success that can be innovated on the fly to achieve maximum profits.

Agents with systems are why the public DISTRUSTS real estate agents, and public opinion regarding real estate agents is ranked with that of used car salesman and attorneys, according to a recent survey from Inman. However, agents who have strategies for success help sellers to prevail with record prices in an ever-competing real estate market.

When looking for a real estate agent, just as I did for this book, read and research. Does the agent have fundamental principles by which their business is built, or do they have a system with a canned script, a PowerPoint presentation that touts their company, and reports of market stats and CMAs? Or, does the agent come and talk to you like a human being, learn what is important to you, and, from that, formulate a strategy for success?

Ask yourself these questions, then make an informed decision; the answer should be clear.

The agent who gave you this book has THAT desire, to help you achieve your goal. IMPACT agents are certified in the Psychological Approach and Fundamental Strategies outlined in the book, and for that reason will help you achieve your desired results.

-Eric Verdi

Table of Contents

7 FUNDAMENTAL STRATEGIES TO SELL YOUR HOME FOR AN ADDITIONAL $30,000

CHAPTER ONE

WHY THIS BOOK

I can't begin to know why you picked up this book. Maybe it was recommended by a friend. Maybe you were unhappy with your real estate agent, or were unsuccessful in selling your home. The title might have caught your eye. Whatever the reason, thank you for choosing to invest your time, your energy, and your money in this book. **I'm grateful.**

Yes, I used the term <u>investing</u>.

Investing will be a common theme throughout this book. Let me be clear. This is NOT a book about real estate investing. This is NOT another "Get-Rich-Quick" guide to real estate. If you are looking for that, look elsewhere!

When I speak of investing throughout this book, I speak of investing in yourself, investing in a different philosophy, and investing in strategies that have helped numerous homeowners put additional profits into their pockets at settlement. Some of these homeowners have shattered neighborhood sales records.

To achieve extraordinary results, you must "Think Differently."

Like Steve Jobs and the wildly successful Apple "Think Differently" campaign, we teach our clients that there is a better, more strategic way to sell your home.

Traditional thinking—what I'll refer to throughout this book as a "price-driven approach"—is taught and practiced by the real estate trainers and companies. This archaic approach has led many sellers down a miserable and unsuccessful path. The IMPACT Approach and strategies outlined in this book, if followed properly, can lead to tremendous results.

This book is a culmination of 14-plus years of real estate experience coupled with decades of studying the buying habits of purchaser and researching human psychology to figure out why a buyer might choose one home over another.

This research was not limited to just home sales. Instead, it was rooted in the psychological patterns we all follow when making the biggest purchase of our lives: our home.

The strategies outlined in this book were gleaned from books like *Influence: The Psychology of Persuasion* by Robert B. Cialdina, PH.D and *The Starbucks Experience: 5 Principles for Turning Ordinary into Extraordinary*. The resulting IMPACT Approach to selling real estate is all about people, because *people* buy homes. They also make decisions on which home to buy on a deeper, emotional level.

But it doesn't end with human psychology. The same sales patterns and motivations can be gleaned from studying successful individuals who built billion-dollar companies on their knowledge of these psychological elements.

These companies GET IT. They understand the product is not what they ultimately sell. They understand products are ever changing; people evolve and industries change. Companies that are built on the backbone of a product ultimately rise and fall with that product.

Companies that are built on a bigger, deeper ideology can adapt as markets change and products revolutionize.

Steve Jobs, Phil Knight, and Howard Schultz. Heard of them? Their companies—Apple, Nike, and Starbucks—are among the most successful in the world.

Apple, Nike, and Starbucks each transcend their product. Think about this for a minute.

Yes, they started off selling computers, sneakers, and coffee. But if their businesses were built around those three products, they would have had a ten-year life cycle and then floundered in mediocrity.

Each company has insanely loyal customers who have built brand loyalty over decades. Jobs, Knight, and Schultz knew early on that the key to success was connecting with customers on a deeper level. I am sure that they committed millions of dollars to researching human psychology and how to best get long-term, loyal customers.

Starbucks is not in the coffee business; they are in the "experience" business.

Think about this: do you go to Starbucks because their $5 coffee is any better than 7-Eleven's or Dunkin Donuts'? No, it is the experience, the barista, the atmosphere. It's a gathering place that has free Wi-Fi and openly welcomes you to come and sit for hours or have business meetings. It's an informal office setting. Howard Schultz realized this from the beginning.

There are five elements outlined in *The Starbucks Experience*, and none have to do with serving coffee. They are all about the customer's experience having a lasting effect. I'll reference these five elements throughout this book. But do yourself a favor and go pick up a copy of *The Starbucks Experience*. It's an easy read but is filled with great insights on business and life.

Phil Knight, the man behind Nike, built an empire and an international brand by promoting dreams.

Nike started in the sneaker business, but has now branched out to include apparel, fashion, and sports equipment, and the company holds sizeable market share in each. How did Knight do this? Not by marketing shoes, because if that were the case, there would have been a ceiling that would have been unbreakable. Remember K-Swiss? Puma? They focused on shoes, and where did that get them? Exactly…

Knight did things differently; he focused on promoting dreams. Two of Nike's famous ad campaigns are "Be Like Mike" and "Just Do It." Everyone remembers these ads—yes, they were used to sell shoes, and later apparel, but the deeper psychological meaning behind these ad campaigns was that if you bought Nike shoes, you would be able to do what Michael Jordan could do. The same thing goes for the "Just Do It" campaign, which focused on starting positive inertia to better your life.

By focusing on people's dreams and a deeper meaning than just selling shoes, Nike grew from a sneaker company into an internationally known brand.

Nike and Starbucks had an influence on my findings and thus played a key role in the development of the IMPACT Approach. But the individual *and company* that blew me away once I started my research were Steve Jobs and Apple.

Steve Jobs was known as an innovator. However, his true genius was his amazing ability to market and create brand loyalty—one that compelled customers to sleep outside his stores for days in anticipation of Apple's latest gadget. How did Jobs do this? One of his most powerful and moving strategies is <u>Story-Telling</u>. He was a master <u>Story-Teller</u>. Jobs had an ability to bring the products that he was about to unveil an almost mythical following before they were even available for sale.

The same lessons can be gleaned from studying the investment strategies of legendary investor Warren Buffett.

Watching so many sellers lose money on their homes and then "fire-sale" their properties, we knew there had to be a superior way for sellers to approach their home sale than the traditional price-driven approach.

What we found was that a home sale, at its core, is no different than a business that is selling a product or a company that is about to go public.

There are specific strategies that companies use when preparing their business for sale. Businesses clean up their balance sheet, eliminate unnecessary expenses, streamline processes, and do what is necessary to increase the value and stock price of their company.

We teach our sellers a similar process that asks them to treat their home like a business with a stock price instead of a home with a sale price.

Before you read the rest of this book and delve into the seven fundamental strategies learned from Steve Jobs and transferred into home sales, it is important to lay the foundation that led to my study of human psychology and why people choose one product over another.

"Price is what you pay. Value is what you get."

Buffett opened our eyes to an entirely new MINDSET about value-investing and how this could translate to helping sellers put up to an additional $30,000 profit in their pockets at settlement.

What is the Warren Buffett Approach to Selling Real Estate?

Have you ever wondered, as I have, "Why must MY house sell for what my neighbor's house down the street sold?" You see, this is what is called a price-driven approach. In this approach, agents base what you can sell or profit from your home on a fixed-priced, based on other similar homes. This is an inferior and outdated approach. I refer to this as an elementary way to sell and price a home. Warren Buffett takes a totally different point of view.

Buffett takes what is called a value-driven approach. He can look at a company's value, NOT its price, and he can find hidden ways to increase the value of that company.

Just like Buffett does with companies, we do with your home. We find ways to increase the value, or better said, the perceived value of your home. This approach is far superior—a value-driven, not a price-driven approach. We do this by hitting emotional triggers with prospective buyers. When buyers can make a decision based on emotion, they are much more likely to make a better offer.

By enhancing the perceived value of their homes, clients have sold their homes for up to $30,000 over similarly priced homes on the market.

Using the combined fundamental strategies learned from The Value-Drive 'Warren Buffet' Approach to Selling Real Estate and the seven psychological factors that Steve Jobs used to build Apple, you give yourself and your home a decided, almost unfair, advantage over the competition.

Imagine watching the 100m race in the Olympics, one of the most watched events every four years during the Summer Games. And one of the runners starts with a 50m lead, an extraordinary advantage. This is similar to how our sellers feel when using the strategies learned from Buffett and Jobs.

There are nine strategies that we teach our clients to increase the value of their home. By applying these nine strategies to their homes, sellers have achieved some amazing results and have broken records for neighborhood sales. Below are two of those strategies.

MORE SHOWINGS MEAN BIGGER PROFITS

Bluntly stated, we want buyers to make emotional decisions, not logical decisions. The more traffic we can generate, meaning more showings, the higher the likelihood of finding that person who doesn't just like your home, but LOVES it. This is why it's important that your home tells a story and captivates potential buyers before they arrive in person.

Here's how we do that: since 92% of homebuyers begin their search for a new home online, photos—what people see about your home—can make or break your success.

7

This is why we hire THE BEST photographer in town, the award-winning Annie Main. What she can do with a camera is incredible. I'm always thrilled when I see other agents out taking their own pictures of the competing homes in a neighborhood with their cheap cameras and poor lighting. The end result is like watching a 1950s black-and-white TV versus today's color TV with crystal clear, stunning high definition. There's NO comparison.

And it's not just the camera and the lighting; once she picks out the best 25 or 30 of those photos, they way they can tell your home's story is nothing short of magic. Sometimes, she takes 200 to 250 different shots to achieve this. I'm not a photographer, so I can't tell you what she does—overlays, stitches, brighten, lightens, whatever it is—but she is a genius at what she does. I'm just honored to have her on my team, using her skills on behalf of my clients. Not long ago, it was proven to me just how powerful her work is and just how big of an effect it really does have.

At a recent showing, we had a female doctor, who lived in southern Maryland. She sent her husband up to view one of my clients' homes. As he was touring the property, I overheard the phone conversation between him and his wife. She asked, "Does the house look anything like the photos?" He assured her that it did.

Within two hours, I had a full-price CASH offer on the home.

It wasn't until a week later that the wife finally laid her eyes on the actual home, and she was still IN LOVE. Now, to be fair, I doubt it was the photos alone that sold this client's home—but, without the photos, I can't help but wonder: *Would this couple have noticed my client's home online? Would my client's home have stood out and captured this couple's attention in the sea of thousands of homes on the Internet?* I don't think so.

This is why we hire Annie to help us (visually) tell your home's story in stunning and vivid full-HD detail, not the outdated 1950s black and-white. Trust me - a photo is not just a photo. And Annie is not cheap. But she is the best. And her ability to tell my clients' homes' stories, time and time again, has proven to yield more showings and thus, bigger profits. I obviously don't know the exact value of extra dollars in profit this represents, as every home is different, but conservatively, an extra $5,000 to $10,000 can pretty easily be expected.

MODEL HOMES GENERATE HIGHER PROFITS

This is a well-known fact. Once buyers can visualize themselves in a home, can see how the layout will work for their family, can feel the openness and love, you have lowered their resistance to making an offer and have also vastly increased the house as their new home, not as one that is lived in by another family, then the buyer will start—as we want them to—to make an emotional decision, not a logical one. And an emotional decision always brings higher profits. This is why—and you may not know this—builders spend so much time studying the science of staging homes correctly. Trust me, little things like this matter.

This is exactly why we hire **THE BEST, MOST SUCCESSFUL** stagers in the area. Have you ever seen the show *Love It or List It?* If not, it's a simple premise. First, there is a homeowner. This homeowner is usually a person who's grown somewhat bored with their home and is now considering selling it. Their partner, however, typically wants to renovate their current home and stay put.

Hilary Farr, the show's interior designer, attempts to restore the homeowner's excitement about their home by "transforming" the current home, while real estate agent David Visentin tries to find them the home of their dreams. Once all renovation work has been completed and all potential homes have been viewed, the couple must decide whether to "love it" or "list it." About 70% of the time, the homeowner chooses to "love it" and remain living there, rather than selling it and moving elsewhere.

This demonstrates how the proper use of **SCIENTIFIC STAGING** can be powerful and can also be a huge motivator in making a buying decision. This works on a behavioral level. Scientific staging pushes buyers from just comparing beds, baths, and square footage to being emotionally connected to a home, in which they can see themselves living. The end result? A higher sales price. This is why we hire stagers on behalf of all of our clients. My stagers, like Hilary Farr, can transform your home from a "lived-in" home that is comfortable and fits your family needs to one that could be mistaken for a model home.

We don't claim to know staging science, so we bring in, locally, the very best.

There is an old adage that says, "You never get a second chance to make a first impression." This is especially true when selling your home. Just as we do with our photographer, Annie Main, we heavily depend on scientific stagers as part of our team to help tell your home's story. The "buzz" that's created from the total package makes your home stand out and leads to quicker, higher-priced sales. And this is not just my opinion. It has been proven. A study by ASP® found that staged homes sold five times faster than non-staged homes. (The average was 29 days for staged homes vs. 145 days for non-staged homes.)

Of course—and it goes without saying—it must be done right; there is a science to this. A lot of real estate agents will claim to be "stagers"—we don't—so be careful and cautious about these claims. We hire stagers on behalf of our clients, and they do it brilliantly.

The ugly part is that for a non-staged home or incorrectly staged home, that additional time on the market (statistics say: an extra 116 days) means that the homeowner is likely to experience one to as many as three price reductions, and typically, most agents push for at least a $5,000 to $10,000 per reduction drop. This can get costly—that's $15,000 to $30,000 in lost profits, not to mention the four extra months of mortgage payments, property taxes, utility and maintenance bills, extra stress, frustration, being inconvenienced, and having people traipse in and out of your home—in your personal space. This is why we operate the way we do and have carefully chosen (and invested in) the team that we have.

Now, paying to transform your home is NOT cheap, but our stagers are worth it, and as a client, this is included. When it comes to your largest investment, as creator and innovator of The Value-Driven Approach to Selling Real Estate, we refuse to cut costly corners. Some agents will and do. Not us. We don't. We refuse. We've seen our clients pocket as much as an additional $10,000 to $15,000 more just from the science of staging alone, which causes buyers to make emotional decisions rather than logical ones. This is the end game and **WE WANT TO WIN!**

If done correctly and strategically, the results are predictable. Do we always break neighborhood records? No. Do we sell every home we list? No. This book is not about a magic formula and promised results. What this book and the fundamental principles in the following pages detail are specific strategies to best position your home against the competition and to have buyers purchase your home as opposed to your neighbor's home down the street.

This Book takes a Story-Based Approach.

The power of a well-told story has an amazing effect on us as humans. Our ancestors passed stories from generation to generation, as this was our main mode of teaching and communication. People might forget the details of presentations and will often forget conversations, but if you can hold their interest through a story, then they'll always remember. Stories have a more powerful and lasting impact.

This book is an easy read, but what you'll learn in the following pages could have a profound impact on you if you are selling your house or any other product or service.

At IMPACT, we have found from clients, friends, and national research that people have a distaste for real estate agents. That is unfortunate, but it is the perception. Hopefully, this book will open your eyes to a new, better way to look at real estate.

So, go grab your favorite beverage—a coffee, coke, tea. Or, if you are reading this in the evening, maybe grab an adult beverage—beer or wine. This book is meant to be fun, but is also meant to educate.

Cheers!!!

CHAPTER TWO

WHY IMPACT?

And no, we don't know where it will lead. We just know there's something much bigger than any of us here. — Steve Jobs

L ike Jobs once said, *"Get closer than ever to your customers. So close that you tell them what they need well before they realize it themselves."*

When it comes to making the biggest investment of your life, you need an agent who thinks about what YOU need to do to sell YOUR home, not how they sold the home down the street. When the "others" offer you their standard, boiler plate presentations, we offer you strategies and customized solutions.

Our agents are trained to do a complete analysis of clients before offering a customized solution. IMPACT agents listen to clients, we learn pain points, we listen to clients' goals and desires. That is why you will never get a 'canned script,' unlike "others" we don't practice scripts, practice how to overcome client objections. In fact, we never "SELL."

If you are a fit for our Approach, you will know. If you are committed to getting your desired results and can put in the work, then you are probably a fit. If you are unwilling to invest in yourself and the process, then you are not the type of client for our Approach.

We recognize that every client has unique needs, goals and desires. Just as Apple taught the world to "Think Differently," at IMPACT we "Do Differently."

One thing you will never get from IMPACT is a cookie cutter approach to selling your home.

Here are 5 ways we set ourselves apart from the "others" of the real estate world and how we create customized solutions for our clients.

1. *We Do NOT Do Listing Presentations*

There's a quote from German philosopher Immanuel Kant that says, "Recognize that human individuals are ends, and do not use them as means to your end."

At IMPACT, we embrace that philosophy 100%. We Don't Sell Homes, We Sell Dreams. Relationships are at the core of everything we do. After all, it is people who make both the buying and selling decisions. And they are more inclined to do so when they're treated as people, rather than cogs in a machine.

There are hundreds – no, thousands - of real estate agents who do not understand this.

They have their MLS listing sales presentations ready to go, with only one end in sight – closing the sale. Most of them mean well (many don't).

At IMPACT, we don't come in with stats and how many sales our company has done. Instead of following the narrow-minded way of the "big" guys of real estate – the guys with their protein shakes, Bluetooth headphones and myopic way of working with clients-we work FOR people.

At IMPACT, we will work *alongside* you to create a story around your home and position your property in an attractive way that meets the unique needs and wants of the buyer.

Instead of following the pattern of "those agents" with their sales pitches and Power Point presentations, we will meet with you and your family. We will start by asking questions, taking notes and listening carefully to your needs and wants.

It starts with a simple fact-finding mission. Every detail and every nuance of your home is discussed. Then – and only then – we will create an experience around your home that your buyers will not be able to resist.

2. *We DO NOT Bait and Switch*

Because we operate on proven and time tested strategies, we don't play the games of "small ball" realtors who bait and switch their clients with small print.

At IMPACT, what you see is what you get. After reading the strategies we lay out in this book, you should have a clear understanding of what we do and why we do it. Because we are so confident in this approach, we also refuse to make small promises.

Marketing guru and sales writer Dan Kennedy makes thousands of dollars for his clients (at least) every time he puts pen to paper. *How does he do this?* He helps himself and his clients stand out from the crowd.

"Take a look at what everyone else in your industry is doing; then do the complete opposite. You'll probably be very successful." – Dan Kennedy, Radical REVENUE

Instead of a "guaranteed" sales program, the only promise we offer is to dig in deep, do our homework and apply our Story-Telling skills to paint your home in the very best light.

In addition to market research, we research your property, its features, history and top selling points, in such detail that we can shine a spotlight on the subtle aspects of your home that distinguish it from all the other homes with *"For Sale"* signs in the yard.

Always be aware of gimmick advertising. If it looks too good to be true, it probably is. That's why our strategies our black and white.

3. *We DO NOT Value Homes Strictly by CMAs*

Remember the Warren Buffett approach to valuing an investment? Just as a company preparing for sale will clean up its books and internal processes to reach a higher closing cost, the home seller can follow a similar pattern to improve the perceived value of their home.

Pricing a home does NOT have to be a tug of war between the agent and the seller. But so often that ends up happening. We see it all the time. An agent immediately wants to do a CMA, or Comparative Market Analysis, and convince the seller that THAT number is what they should hope to earn from the sale.

Meanwhile, the seller wants to get as much as possible from their initial investment.

The seller understands their home has value – that it offers unique features and distinctly valuable assets that a formula could never measure.

The price-driven model to home sales is an Inferior Approach.

Warren Buffett understand how to enhance and increase perceived value, and it's something we embrace at IMPACT. Not only do we understand the value-driven approach, but we know how to USE it to get a buyer to pay MORE than the CMA.

Value – not price – is our end game because when a buyer sees value in a new purchase, they are willing to throw their 'estimated values' from Zillow.com or Redfin.com out of the window.

Of course, we do use your home's CMA as a starting point. But it is never used to create a final evaluation.

We move beyond the first price evaluation and archaic Price-Driven approach to look for hidden ways to improve the perceived value of your property.

At IMPACT, we understand that price benefits are superficial, and to get the most out of your investment, our time and energy is better spent creating an emotional attachment for the purchaser. **The Psychological Approach was carefully developed with that goal in mind.**

4. We DO NOT Self Promote

I once knew a real estate agent from D.C. who plastered her own pictures and gold logo over every piece of material she sent her clients and prospects.

From newsletters to self-promotional CD's, postcards and email campaigns, that logo and her face was all you could see.

You know what you couldn't see? Client testimonials? Stories of the homes she sold or examples of happy sellers who got more than they expected from working with her? (I won't say her name here, of course, but it was a great example of how I DID NOT want to run my own real estate business).

At IMPACT, we agree with the words of marketer Scott Cook who said, "A brand is not what we tell the consumer it is – it is what consumers tell each other it is."

That's why we will never make the business of selling your home about us. You won't see our names or faces slapped across shiny billboards or postcards. It's not about us – it's about our approach and how we achieve greater profits for our clients.

Our testimonials speak for themselves. We don't have to do self-promotions. Instead, we invest in every home we sell because we believe it we treat our clients well and work hard to earn them more profits from their sale, they will tell our story for us.

5. We DO NOT Nickel and Dime Our Clients

A few years ago, when most U.S. airlines were struggling to stay afloat and losing money by the truckload, they made decisions that ended up separating them as wheat from the proverbial chaff.

They started charging fees for bags. It was a "brilliant" idea from airline CEOs who wanted to offset their losses. But it backfired. You can see it now by looking at the slow decline in ticket purchases on airlines like Frontier, American or Delta.

Nickle and diming clients doesn't build a successful brand. It's a desperate, last-ditch effort that inevitably weakens an organization's entire business model.

But not all airlines went down that path. Southwest Airlines, for example, was determined to be different. They became the "no frills" provider that offered to do just one simple thing: get you where you needed to go ON TIME.

They created an entire philosophy around their simplistic approach called "TransFAREncy," which they define as the "philosophy created by Southwest Airlines® in which customers are treated honestly and fairly, and low fares actually stay low—no unexpected bag fees, change fee, or hidden fees. Created and practiced exclusively by Southwest Airlines."

We might not be selling airline tickets, but at IMPACT, we follow the pattern of Southwest. They're transparent in their fares; we're transparent in our commissions.

Our agents will never charge you an admin or transactional fee. In fact, we believe real estate agents who do that probably don't feel that highly about their own skills to sell homes at a fair price to begin with.

It's against the core of our character to charge a few hundred dollars on a transactional fee when we're earning a commission. We NEVER do it.

Our commissions are enough. Our faith is in our strategies and the work we do to increase the value of your home. If we've done that, we've done our job. The rest will take care of itself.

CHAPTER THREE

WHY STEVE JOBS

I n 2007, Steve Jobs was *Time Magazine's* "Person of the Year." But his real gift was never fully understood. Steve Jobs is labeled as a visionary. But as a marketer, he may have been the best the world has ever seen.

I've seen a lot of homes that fail to sell. It's never a pretty process. Homeowners get disheartened and frustrated. They often feel deceived by their agent. Maybe they were promised a certain outcome or a quick sale at a certain price point, but then they fail to deliver. So, I can understand these homeowners' frustrations. It's also, though, why I asked that question in response to my fascination with seeing Steve Jobs do what he did...

...Sell millions upon millions of gadgets

Steve Jobs used human psychology, not fancy marketing or promotion, to sell tens of millions of iPhones, iPods, and iPads! And he did it at premium prices. What if his secret could be applied to selling real estate?

I mean, seriously, what if Steve Jobs' secret—the understanding of human psychology, the intricacies of the human mind, how it works, processes information, and how it makes decisions—could be applied to selling real estate?

To Steve Jobs, a house, like a phone, is just a product. It's an opportunity—I think he would say—to impact someone's life in a significant and meaningful way.

So why can't the Steve Jobs method be applied to real estate? Do the same psychological processes, decision-making, and value-proposition principles not apply?

Carmine Gallo, the author of *The Presentation Secrets of Steve Jobs*, provides a number case studies that outline Jobs' methods in full detail and how he uses psychology to get a buyer from Point A to Point B. If you haven't already read it, I suggest you pick up a copy.

Our agents at IMPACT have consumed this book and many more like it, each one deepening our understanding, thinking and appreciation of these more sophisticated sales methods.

Most real estate agents don't really think much about preparing or pricing a home. Sure, they go through the motions. But they use very standard ideas, mostly from an archaic approach.

But it doesn't have to be that way.

Just think, "What if, instead of treating a home like a property with a sales price, you treated it like a business with a stock price? What if you prepared it for sale as an investment firm would a private business that was set to go public?"

At IMPACT, we have been using what we have uncovered in our research for years now. Our clients have greatly benefited. They love it *and the results*. They simply know it as "The Warren Buffett Approach to Selling Real Estate." In fact, since 2014, using this approach in five different neighborhoods, we've broken the price-per-square-foot record, each time contributing a significant *additional* profit for our clients.

It's not unusual to see additional profits that total up to $30,000 or more—that is, if the client will follow the strict directions laid out for them. You know how it is, though—some people just can't seem to listen…

But this brings me back to Steve Jobs. You see, the Warren Buffett question—that was then. This is now. And if you're not innovating or trying to push the limits of what is possible in terms of profit, selling real estate, or whatever, then I believe you're settling. And we never want to settle, not when it comes to our clients. Settling would be disrespectful. Resting on his laurels is never how Steve Jobs did things, either.

In regards to human psychology, here is one of the seven triggers we discovered that Jobs used repeatedly…

STORYTELLING.

Pretty much everyone understands what that is. *The concept.* But few *truly* understand, as Jobs did, how it applies to the marketing of a product or service, or what effect it has, or what positive impact it can make on the way people assign value to things.

Perhaps the best example of the power of Storytelling can be found in looking at the case study of the…egg whisk.

The amazing egg whisk. Purchased for 25 cents. Sold for $30. The power of *STORY.*

In researching the success of storytelling and how it can relate to selling products or services, I came across a fantastic website, SignificantObjects.com. The site describes itself as "a literary and anthropological experiment devised by Rob Walker and Joshua Glenn, demonstrated that the effect of narrative [story] on any given object's subjective value can be measured objectively." Walker and Glenn hypothesized that they could take any mundane object, have a writer tell a compelling story about that object, and then sell the object attached to the story at an increased value.

Here's how the experiment worked: they would first obtain objects from thrift stores and garage sales. These objects would cost no more than a few bucks, and some were even free. The next step of the experiment had a writer create a short story about the object. The final step was selling the "junk" items on eBay; the only difference between when they curated the item and when they sold it was that a story was now attached to the item.

The results of this experiment were amazing!

The researchers purchased $128.74 worth of thrift-store "junk." They attached a story to each item and sold them for an astounding $3,612.51. What they found was that the power of a story raised the perceived value of the items by 2,806%! For example, an old egg whisk was purchased for 25 cents and sold on eBay for $30 after the whisk's "story" was told.

From this experiment, the researcher hypothesis was 100% accurate.

Stories create an emotional attachment to a product for consumers, and a story told the right way can add significant value to even the most insignificant items—even an egg whisk.

Walker and Glenn concluded that "stories are such a powerful driver of emotional value that their effect on any given object's subjective value can actually be measured objectively." Or simply put, "When someone likes a story about an object—or your home, if it's on the market and you're selling—that emotional connection is expressed by the buyer's willingness to pay a higher sales price." This, of course, earns the seller of the object a greater profit.

This is what made Steve Jobs the ultimate marketer. He knew that humans create an emotional, almost religious, attachment to products through the power of story.

When Apple would release a new product, it was Jobs who would do a product unveil to the public. This huge unveiling would typically take place in front of a live audience near the conclusion of Macworld. (Macworld is an annual international tradeshow dedicated to the Apple/Mac platform.)

Each year, anticipation would grow as the date got closer to see what Apple and Jobs would be unveiling that year.

Jobs was a master *Storyteller* and would take the audience on an emotional journey throughout the unveiling until the audience was bursting at the seams, waiting to hear the conclusion and thus, see the new product.

The best example of the power of story occurred during the 2007 Macworld, when Jobs unveiled the iPhone. Leading up to the event, no one knew what Apple was going to introduce. There were rumors, blog posts, and articles speculating what was going to be released, but no one knew for sure. Jobs used this mystique during his speech. (Google, "Steve Jobs introduces the iPhone" and watch for yourself.)

Jobs tells the audience that Apple is introducing three products—three revolutionary products. He starts by talking about all of Apple's innovations throughout the years—the Mac computer, the iPod, etc.

He then does the product unveiling for the year. In a drawn-out story, Jobs says, "The first product is a widescreen iPod with touch controls. [The crowd cheers loudly]. Second is a revolutionary mobile phone. [The crowd cheers even louder]. And the third is a breakthrough internet communications device. [Tepid cheers]." He then tells the audience, "These are not three separate devices, and these are all in one device…the iPhone. Today, we are reinventing the phone. [The crowd jumps out of their seats]."

This perfectly scripted *STORY* is the reason why Jobs always had the media buzzing in anticipation. Buyers were stalking stores and camping out. Consumers felt such a connection—through story—that they HAD to have Apple's latest product.

Storytelling **is one of the main strategies that Jobs employed to build Apple.**

In total, there are seven fundamental strategies that Steve Jobs utilized to become one of the best marketers the world has ever seen. Throughout this book, you will learn each of the seven strategies being key to Jobs' success; and thus, we have engineered them to apply to success in real estate.

You see, stories are what people remember best. Most real estate agents will spew statistics about themselves or give you a lame PowerPoint presentation. What these agents don't understand—and what Steve Jobs understood so well—is that what really emotionally connects consumers to a product is a well told story. When you become a *storyteller*, you become powerful; you can create value for yourself and your home.

CHAPTER FOUR

FUNDAMENTAL STRATEGY #1

Story-Selling

"Don't Sell Homes; Sell Dreams"

"If history were taught in the form of stories, it would never be forgotten." –Rudyard Kipling

T hat quote 100% applies to selling real estate, too. "If homes were described in the form of stories, they would never be forgotten." It's just the way human behavior is.

We're hardwired to listen to and fall in love with stories. Once you connect with a cause, a product, a person, or a home on a deeper level—thanks to the power of story—your commitment to it is strengthened and solidified. By creating a strong emotional attachment for buyers to your home, you eliminate their barriers to purchase.

Since this book is about how to maximize your profits when selling your home, the industry on which I'm going to focus is real estate. I want to show you exactly how this can be done.

But the lessons and principles within this book could be applied to any industry, be it selling a product or service.

Just think about it. Emotional attachment is a special thing, and you see it everywhere. It could be a sports team—buying a jersey and investing three hours watching a game makes one become emotionally invested in that team. Or, it might be a cause—curing cancer, for example. If you or a loved one has battled cancer, you immediately become emotionally invested in finding a cure. Or, how about a person? Every four years, the public becomes emotionally connected to their favorite candidate when electing a new President. They put up signs in their yards, have bumper stickers on their cars, and try to influence friends that are "on the fence." They are emotionally invested in that candidate. And all of this emotional investment is mainly because of the "stories" that are playing in our minds.

Because of this emotional attachment, you overlook the flaws that others may see in that person, product, or team because you are invested.

How can you create an emotional attachment to a home?

You can do this the same way that Steve Jobs built Apple into the most valuable company in the world. The underlying message that Jobs conveyed every time he spoke—and he believed this—was that you, the consumer, would be better because you owned an Apple product.

Strip down all the fancy marketing, all the promotions, the fancy gadgets, and the constant breakthroughs in technology.

EVERY time that Jobs went out to sell a new product, he didn't focus on the PRODUCT itself; he focused on its BENEFIT. And he wrapped and presented that benefit in the form of a story.

In a *Washington Post* article by Michael O'Sullivan, titled *"Filmmaker Alex Gibney on Steve Jobs, Storyteller,"* O'Sullivan asks this question of Jobs: "What was he at heart? A Storyteller. That's what his genius was—telling us all a story. His artistry was in

30

telling the kind of story that we would believe, telling us a story to make us want something."

Jobs didn't bore consumers with the mechanics of how the product worked. Frankly, NO ONE CARED. All consumers care about is what BENEFIT they are going to derive from that product.

The major breakthrough of the iPod was actually the computing technology that dramatically increased memory on a physically smaller scale. But when introducing the iPod, Jobs focused on having 1,000 songs in your pocket. And he only revealed that punch line after first weaving ten minutes of an incredible tale.

Sure, Steve Jobs was the CEO of a tech company. But it was the power of story that sold 37 million iPhones, a gazillion iPods, iPads, etc.

When selling your home, take a page out of the playbook of Steve Jobs and come up with the benefits of owning your home (as opposed to the one down the street.)

Instead of focusing on the minor details of the home and every insignificant feature, focus on the BENEFIT to the purchaser. Then, figure out how to appropriately present that benefit.

This is accomplished by properly telling your home's story.

At IMPACT, STORY is the fundamental strategy we use to distinguish one home over another. Once a potential buyer reads the stories we create, they never forget the home.

The rest of this book and the other fundamental strategies all build upon the story. You can't have the "Hero vs. Villain"

(*Strategy #4*) if you don't first establish the framework of a powerful story. The "Rule of Threes" (*Strategy #2*) also means *nothing* outside of the story framework.

After much research and several years of experimentation, at IMPACT, we discovered that Warren Buffett's value-driven approach to investing and Steve Jobs' storytelling approach CAN be applied to real estate. And, when combined, they WILL help our clients make significantly greater gains.

Following a nine-step process, we position your home in the best light possible to be able to achieve maximum return.

The Warren Buffett Approach is done before the home is even listed—a necessary step if you want to extract maximum profit. Some sellers take two to three months to properly prepare their home for sale. Others take three weeks.

While preparing your home properly can be a pain, it is an absolute necessity if you're going to achieve the highest return. Without this step, you could hit every psychological trigger but still be at a disadvantage.

The next step is to properly tell the story. First, tell it visually. Second, tell it through the most powerful form of communication—the written word.

Follow one step without the other, and you will lose 65% of attention from potential buyers, a point confirmed by a study conducted by Dr. Richard Mayer of the University of California.

Both words and pictures, when combined, increase retention rates of the viewer by 65%. Therefore, using both kinds of media is imperative to selling your home for maximum profit. (*After all, if we can't capture and hold the attention of potential buyers who view dozens of properties, then your home will be forgotten.)*

In the next chapter, we will introduce the Psychology behind the "Rule of Threes" and how the human mind retains information. There is a specific step we take so that buyers remember your home over all others.

And rather than explaining the minutia of how this is done, Exhibits 1.1 to 1.3 demonstrate how this Story-Selling concept has been carried out for several past clients.

Further, here are the results of past clients, in their own words, who have utilized this approach.

–After one of our [IMPACT] agents sent a copy of a property story to a seller, she replied, "Wow, sounds amazing! Makes me teary-eyed and want to stay! (Just kidding.) I love it!"

- Keith said, "[IMPACT] is a small personable company. They pay full attention to their clients' needs. They put forth full efforts to accommodate the need of their clients. Most of all, Eric and Marla are both wonderful and honest individuals and it was my pleasure to meet them both."

- Patrick T. said, "Being first-time sellers and relocating out of the area during the sale of our home, we were very worried and scared that we would not be able to handle this process appropriately and would burn additional resources. [Our agent] provided the best strategy, kept us informed, and ultimately, closed the deal in a very short time period. [IMPACT] got it done!"

Exhibit 1.1

There is History on This Here Lane...

Let's go back in time. Imagine the Hatfields and McCoys building a church together because their children are about to marry. Well, this actually happened in Buckeystown around the turn of the century—not the Hatfields and McCoys, but two prominent families. The story you are about to read has been passed down by generations of residents on "The Lane."

Are you tired of driving through all the neighborhoods that have sprouted up all over the area? You know the ones I'm talking about. Where builders offer you three or four choices of homes and then you can choose your elevation to make your home "look different." Who are they fooling? All the houses are basically the same.

If you desire something different, something unique, something with character and history, then you've hit the jackpot. 6823 Buckingham Lane was built in 1898; however, it was recently completely renovated and expanded, keeping a period-specific feel but with modern finishings. Priced about the same as the cookie-cutter townhomes, however, on "The Lane," you get your own home, own fenced backyard, and a piece of history for $349,900.

Maybe Buckingham Lane won't work for you, but I guarantee that if you see it for yourself, you won't be disappointed. The owners have done a fabulous job modernizing and expanding this turn-of-the-century homestead.

The Story Told By Generations...

The late 1800s and early 1900s were a different era. Only a couple generations ago, times were slower—the automobile was just starting to take over from the horse and buggy, and America was being built on factories and manufacturing.

Buckeystown was no different. With access to waterways and a railroad, and located about 45 miles from both Washington DC and Baltimore, there were two thriving industries in Buckeystown. One was built on the natural resources found in the fertile ground; the other was manufacturing. The two companies dominated the local landscape and employment in Buckeystown, but were both also vital to the development of housing in the area.

Owning a Piece of History

That is the where the history of "The Lane" started. The neighbors and the residents of Buckeystown just refer to Buckingham Lane as simply "The Lane," something that I didn't know until I met Jennifer and Matt (the sellers of this beautiful home), and they told me the story.

Back around the turn of the century, when the homes on The Lane were being built for the workers in the area, there were two classes living on the street, and this is still apparent from the structures today. The homes on the left side of the street are larger and built of brick. This is where the "supervisors" lived; it was their side of the street. The homes on the right of The Lane were modest in size and housed the "workers"—definitely a sign of a different era.

Then the story goes that the church at the end of The Lane in Buckeystown was built by the heads of the two families that ran the industries, because their son and daughter were getting married and they needed a church for the ceremony. And you thought weddings today were expensive?! The wedding was a grand event, and nearly all the residents of Buckeystown attended.

Homes are not just places to eat, sleep, and raise your family. When they are historic, there is a certain vibe, a certain ambiance that you know the home holds, as it has been passed from one generation to the next. The Bobbitts are only the third owners of 6823 Buckeystown Lane; will you be the fourth?

Let's Talk About the Home

Pulling up to 6823 on "The Lane," the first thing that will catch your eye is the beautiful celadon siding, and the bright white trim is a stunning contrast in color that promotes a warm and inviting feel. The exterior siding has been totally redone with Hardiplank. Walking up the four steps of the new front porch to the front door, you can feel the pride of craftsmanship with the remodel.

Opening the front door, there are two features that immediately POP and attract your attention. The first are the hardwood floors throughout the home, also tastefully restored. The second is a brick structure in between the living room and the dining room. This used to be the main fireplace used to heat the entire home.

As you walk through the dining room, you will come to the new section of the home that includes a kitchen, eat-in, family room combination. The kitchen is stunning with upgraded cabinets, granite counters, and a breakfast bar area. On the opposite wall is room for your less formal but more utilized kitchen table. On the rear wall opposite of the entrance to the dining room is a wood-burning fireplace. A brick surround with a natural wood mantel brings you back to a peaceful, more relaxing time when families gathered around the fire, playing board games or reading together.

Imagine spending a chilly fall evening or winter snowstorm next to the fireplace, with the wood crackling as you sit and sip on hot chocolate and read your favorite novel as you watch the beautiful nature in your rear yard. Cozy.

Let's Head Upstairs

Heading up the staircase to the second floor; you can imagine how many times people have made this tract upstairs over the last 117 years. At the top of the stairs is a full bathroom. Completely redone, this bath services both the second and third bedrooms. The upstairs flooring in the hall and both bedrooms is the original hardwood flooring, similar to downstairs.

Walking down the hallway to the master bedroom is a transformation in time from the original house to the new addition built a few years ago. Except for a few subtle differences (new hardwood), it is tough to tell that this is an addition, as the owners have done a masterful job of making everything feel period-specific.

The master suite is off the rear of the home over the kitchen and family room and is 18 feet by 16 feet, large enough for your bedroom furniture. There are dual closets that allow both to have their own separate space. The master bath also has dual sinks and a separate shower area. The flooring has been upgraded to oversized ceramic tile.

Your Own Private Oasis

The rear of the home is perfect for entertaining. Off the kitchen area are two 15-panel glass doors that open to your oasis. The deck starts on the side of the home and is about 9 feet by 12 feet on the side…but there is more. On the rear of the home in a continuous connection is a rear deck that is roughly 20 feet by 18 feet. You could literally have all the neighbors from "The Lane" over to your home and host them on your deck! The rest of the rear yard includes a play set area. It is totally fenced-in, so if you have a dog or other animals, they can run freely in the rear yard. Near the back of the yard is a shed that is ideal for storing your mower, yard equipment, bikes, canoe, etc

Oh yeah, one feature that I forgot to mention that is unique: the basement area has been finished and can be used as a recreation-type room to just hang and relax. It really has an awesome feeling, as the stone foundation has been sealed and your walls are stones. Pretty Cool.

Ask Yourself This...

If you could own a piece of history that has been totally remodeled and expanded to fit your needs—one that is unique and doesn't have the cookie-cutter feel of the new planned neighborhoods, where the finishing's and attention to detail have been custom-made for this home—how much would you be willing to pay? The price is attractive at $349,900, as townhouses just a few miles away are going for similar prices. Come take a tour; you won't be disappointed.

If you are already working with an agent, call them to schedule your own private showing.

Exhibit 1.2

Grandeur rarely seen by a track builder...

When looking for your "forever" home, do you want cookie-cutter or do you want something with style, class, and its own flavor? If you desire a home that stands out above the crowd, then you might have just found it. Read the story, check out the tour, and decide for yourself.

Have you been looking for just the right home but have been disappointed in what you have seen on the market? Maybe it wasn't large enough, maybe you didn't like the lot, or maybe it needed updating that you didn't want to do. If you have been disappointed in what you have seen for sale, I'd suggest that you do yourself a favor and check out 9327 Hillsborough Drive in Spring Ridge.

You get a 5,287 square foot home (according to a recent appraisal) on three finished levels. This is a beautiful brick front home on a corner lot with a three-car garage and a massive deck overlooking the woods.

Discover the Difference

As Spring Ridge was being built in the 1990s and early 2000s, there were different builders throughout the years that built here. Quite frankly, the neighborhood had so many homes being built in it that it was too large of a project for just one builder. This is good, in that not all of the homes are exactly the same or some variation of the same floor plan from house to house.

The massive home at 9327 Hillsborough Drive was built near the end of the building that took place for the single family homes in Spring Ridge, and the builder at this time was Ryan Homes. Ryan offers many different models, but one of their most impressive is the "Waverly Model." The base Waverly already comes with upgrades as part of the basic package, but the original owners still added some additional features, making Hillsborough stand out.

Three Features Rarely Seen in Spring Ridge

The first upgrade that you'll notice when pulling up is that there is a three-car garage, complete with a workbench nook. I have only seen a handful of others in Spring Ridge that come with a three-car garage. The advantage here is obvious. If you have three cars, then all of them can be in the garage, or if you are like me and need additional storage, a three-car garage is priceless. You can park both of your vehicles in the garage and STILL have room for storage so that you are not taking anything away from the living area in your home.

Second is the corner lot. This feature is also obvious as to why it's unique for Spring Ridge, because there are only so many corner lots that can be built in any neighborhood. The advantage here is that you have a nearly .40-acre lot, which is on the larger end for Spring Ridge. Plus, because of its location within the neighborhood, the home backs onto a wooded area that, in the summer, is full of bloom and bright colors; so instead of backing onto a neighbor's home, you get a great view of a quiet wooded area.

The third distinguishing feature is a double staircase from the main living level to the upper level. An option in this model was to add dual staircases, and the original owner did just that. So, not only do you have the traditional staircase when you first enter the foyer that leads to the upstairs, but you have a second (back) staircase off the family room that leads to the upstairs as well.

Just these three features alone make 9327 Hillsborough Drive a unique find for Spring Ridge, but there are many more that make this lovely home POP.

First Impressions Are Everything

So, with the side-loading three-car garage, you, as the homeowner, will most likely enter the living area of your home through the garage. Entering the living area through the garage, you will come through a dual purpose room. The first is a mudroom/coat room where you can come in and take off your shoes, jacket, and put down any personal belongings you may be bringing home. The second function of this room is that it serves as the laundry room with a washer and dryer. From there, you'll enter the home just off the kitchen area.

Now, most of your guests will come around to your main/front entrance. Well-cared-for and beautifully landscaped, your new home has great "curb appeal." The other feature that makes 9327 Hillsborough stand out is that is sits ever so slightly on a hill, so this makes an already large home seem massive in appearance. Plus, the red brick front pops against the backdrop of a beautiful blue sky.

Now, Let's Take a Tour of the Interior

The first thing that you'll notice as you enter the front door is the grand appearance of the interior of Hillsborough. To your left, through French doors, is your own home office/study that is perfect for today's professional who either works from home or is allowed to have remote office days.

Enter the front door and to your right is even more impressive—there are two well-appointed rooms that are accompanied by very nice hardwood flooring. The formal living room and the dining room are both 15 feet by 12 feet, so you'll never feel cramped when entertaining family or guests. The dining room is accentuated with crown molding, chair railing, and decorative trim work.

Making your way down the hall from the front door is an extra-large (18' by 13') kitchen with granite counters and a large island that is perfect for baking, cooking, or serving meals, as there is enough of an overhang for two or three people to eat. The owners have also added the bump-out off the back of the house from the kitchen, so you also have an 18' x 9' "morning room." Most people use this as the regular eat-in area, but I have seen some owners use this area as a sitting area—more of the "Florida" feel. These five rooms—office, living room, dining room, kitchen, and morning room—all have hardwood flooring.

The last room on the main living level is the regularly used family room. You take one step down from the kitchen into this 19 foot by 18-foot living area. The opposite wall features a gas-burning fireplace and a cathedral ceiling, making this massive room seem even larger. On the back side of the family room is the second/back staircase.

Heading Upstairs

Another distinguishing feature of 9327 Hillsborough Drive is that the second-floor hallway and all four bedrooms have hardwood flooring. The master suite is off the back staircase and is quite large itself, with a 21' by 20' footprint. Off to one side is currently used as a sitting room, where you can relax and read on your couch after a hard day's work, or you can watch your favorite TV show as you prepare for bed.

Got a lot of clothes? Like a large closet? There are dual closets in the master suite, and the first time I was there, I almost mistook the larger walk-in closet as a bowling alley! Seriously, if you run out of room in this closet, you might be related to Imelda Marcos.

The master bath features dual sinks, a soaking tub, and a separate shower.

The other three bedrooms and full bath are down the hall. Each bedroom is ample-sized, and you'll never have the cramped feeling of a smaller track home.

Fully Finished Lower Level

In case the upstairs living area wasn't enough home for you, there is a fully finished (about 1,700 square feet) walkout basement. There is a fully renovated spa-like bath that would be perfect for showers or freshening up after you get done working out in your exercise room.

What you get in your lower level is: a separate exercise room, another nice-sized 14' x 10' room that is currently set up as a guest bedroom (but I can't advertise it as a bedroom because of its lack of an egress), a large media room that can be used to entertain guests or just as a separate hangout for family members, then there is a large finished open space on the other side of the basement that could be a den/play area/extra office. Additionally, plumbing has been run to accommodate a wet bar that would make this the ultimate "man cave."

Now…Let's Take a Walk Outside

Remember that morning room off the kitchen? There is a door from the morning room to the rear deck. And this is not just any deck—we are talking impressive. Low-maintenance decking is 42 feet by 25 feet and includes built-in seating. You could easily accommodate a party for your entire street on this rear deck. Off the back of the home is your wooded area.

There is truly no stone left unturned in this beautiful, massive home.

Act Now, Before You Miss Out…

The price is $519,900. Here is what you get for that price. A large corner lot in the "new" section of Spring Ridge, a beautiful brick front home with a three-car garage, and 5,287 square feet of finished space on three levels. Definitely not your cookie-cutter home. Sales in Spring Ridge have been brisk since mid-2014.

If you want to have all the amenities of living in a planned community, plus have one of the most impressive, largest, and unique homes, then look no further. Come check out our 9327 Hillsborough Drive for yourself, and you won't be disappointed.

If you are already working with an agent, call them to schedule your own private showing.

Exhibit 1.3

Luxury and Comfort Form the Perfect Match…

A Perfect 10! Four immaculately finished levels that include six bedrooms, five full baths, and one half bath. Must see pictures and tour to appreciate. Gourmet-style kitchen, home office, wet bar, "man cave" in basement, double view fireplace. Enormous master suite with incredible walk-in closets, additional storage, and top-of-the-line bath. Back of home has

49

stone paver patio that backs to wooded area. $700,000.

If you have been looking for a home that WOWs you upon entering and then continues to exceed your expectations as you tour the entire home, then you need not look any further. Box Turtle Court was built in 2008 with every upgrade imaginable, and the finishings and enhancements that the sellers have made in that time make Box Turtle an over-the-top home. I guarantee that if you schedule a private showing, you will not be disappointed.

Lake Linganore may not work for everyone, but if you desire community amenities that include trails, three swimming pools, a beach on the lake, tennis courts, etc., then you may have just found the right home.

Fascinating Story

Every home has unique features that, ultimately, make the owners think their homes stand out amongst the competition and make their home "the best in the neighborhood." Most owners are misguided, not intentionally, by a term that psychologists have named the Self Valuation Principal. What this means is that once

you own something, you hold it in higher regards than do others, because you have emotional attachment and sentimental value in that product. Unfortunately, when selling a home, it is nearly impossible to get a buyer to pay above value for a home because you have emotional attachment, unless you TRULY do have the best home in the neighborhood.

Then, the opposite happens via the Contrast Principal that I recently wrote about in an article I published. To read that article, go to www.EricVerdiProperties.com.

The premise is that when buyers are out looking at homes, you must make your home standout against other homes on the market. And if you can make it stand out positively, then the difference will be exaggerated in a positive position. What this means to the seller is higher profits and greater ROI when selling.

Having been in multiple of hundreds of homes in Lake Linganore throughout the last decade, from new construction to original homes to lakefront, I have seen pretty much everything in the area and I can say, unequivocally, that Box Turtle is the most impressive home I've entered.

Grandeur at Its Finest

Pulling onto Box Turtle Court off of Accipter, you will notice the impressive homes on this court. Your neighbors have the pride of ownership that you desire when purchasing a home of this stature. 6720 will be on your left as you are pulling down the court. The home is perched on a hill and makes the four levels of living even MORE impressive.

Around the rear of the home is a peaceful setting that even features a stone paver patio area that is perfect for those summer cookouts and neighborhood parties.

Then, when you pull into the driveway, two features will immediately catch your eye. First, there is a three-car garage. And second, you'll notice that three of the sides are brick, but once you walk around back, you'll find that all four sides are brick—an upgrade that is not typical of the homes built today and is an added luxury. Remember the story of the Three Little Pigs and the Big, Bad Wolf? There is a reason that they ended up in the brick home. Making your way up the steps to the front door, you are in anticipation of what awaits.

First Impressions Are EVERYTHING

Open the front door and your eyes are immediately drawn to the boldness and large open room. To your right is the "bourbon room"—others might call it the formal living room, but the owners have made this a very chill sitting room that is perfect for sitting and relaxing and having a bourbon or two after a long day's work. Through the bourbon room is a large 18-foot by 13-foot dining room, complete with crown molding. The top two-thirds of the wall is a soft blue, and the bottom third is accentuated with bright white paint, completed with shadow box trim.

Back to the front door, immediately to your left as you enter the home is an office/study room that has an entire wall with a built-in bookcase. This room is the ideal sitting room/office, as it overlooks the bottom half of Aspen.

Making your way down the hall, you will come to the kitchen, which is the focal point of every home, but the magnificent kitchen at Box Turtle is beyond approach. It features top-of-the-line stainless steel appliances that include a double oven and a four-burner stainless gas cooktop on the main island. Speaking of the island, it is granite and has a breakfast-bar-height counter that comfortably seats four. Imagine having your friends over on a Friday night for dinner. While you are cooking your favorite meal, your guests are seated on the other side of the bar sipping their favorite cocktail as you plan your next vacation getaway.

Just off of the kitchen is an eat-in area that would be perfect for your kitchen table. The area is large enough to comfortably fit an oversized eight-seat rectangular table.

One Step Down to Luxury

Coming off the kitchen area, you take one step down to the main family room, which is adorned with hardwood flooring, plenty of natural light from side and rear windows, and a double-sided gas fireplace—enough room for just about any furnishings, at 20' by 17'.

Yes, I mentioned the double-sided fireplace—well, on the other side of the family room is an additional family/sitting room. This room also has plenty of natural light, as it has windows on the front and the side of the house, and again has hardwood flooring. I don't have the exact measurements of this particular level, but I walked it off the other day, and there is about 2,400 square feet of living area on this level.

I forgot to mention that the finishings, paint, and moldings are incredible. The first floor has hardwood throughout.

Enough Room for the Largest of Families

Making your way upstairs to the "main" upper level, you'll again notice the grandeur of Box Turtle. To your right are two ample-sized bedrooms at 13' x 12' and 12' x 12', but what makes them stand out is that they have their own Jack and Jill bath. This is ideal for those who want direct access to the bathroom without having to enter the hall.

If you come to the top of the steps and make a slight turn to your left, the fourth and fifth bedrooms are on the left and right respectively. These are both nicely appointed and offer a level of comfort not typically seen in today's construction. The bath for these two bedrooms is a hall bath located just outside of the fourth bedroom. The current owners use the fifth bedroom as an office, and a custom feature that they had the builder include to this room was to have the laundry put in an oversized closet in the fifth bedroom. This way, the laundry is on the same level as the bedrooms.

Luxury Sleeping at Its Finest

Walking down the hall to the master bedroom, you'll open the door and feel like you are walking into a king's suite. The master is ginormous, at 23' x 17', but it feels even larger because of its vaulted ceiling and bump-out sitting room on the front of the house. The owners have installed two additional closets in the front dormers to give you additional storage or closet space.

The original closet is a massive walk-in that is roughly 12' x 10' and should be enough room for even the most fashion-conscious individuals.

Stepping into the master bath is the equivalent of walking into a five-star hotel. It features beautiful tile work, separate soaking tub

and shower with tile surround, and dual sinks. Make sure you check out the pictures, as the view from the bath out to the rear is amazing and peaceful.

When All You Want is to Get Away

Remember those famous infomercials? The ones that say, "But wait, there's more." Well, it holds true for Box Turtle; there is more. Make your way up to the second "upstairs," the third level. Upon entering the upper level, there is another bedroom with full bath and an additional sitting room or office. This could be another owner's suite, or might be ideal to give guests their own private space, or maybe a perfect place for the teenaged child to have their private space.

Fully Finished Lower Level

Heading down to the lower level off of the kitchen, you enter a very chill lower level, complete with a fully finished wet bar and media room. There is another full bath that, like the others, is done to the nines. Box Turtle is truly an amazing home and must be seen to be fully appreciated.

Don't Hesitate or You'll Miss Out

The price is $700,000. The features included in this home are worth the price, and the grandness of this home that include 5,421 square feet of finished space (according to tax records) make this an appealing alternative to what is currently on the market.

New Market and, in particular, the Aspen subdivision of Lake Linganore is a desirable location with all the amenities that Lake Linganore has to offer. Do yourself a favor and make sure that you check out 6720 Box Turtle Court—you will NOT be disappointed.

CHAPTER FIVE

FUNDAMENTAL STRATEGY #2

The Rule of Three

"Today, we are introducing THREE revolutionary products." – Steve Jobs

This is what Steve Jobs announced to Macworld in 2007 as he introduced the revolutionary iPhone. In a product unveiling that changed the world, Jobs knew exactly what he was doing as he initially introduced the iPhone as three separate devices. Separate, they were an MP3 player, a phone, and an internet communicator. He sang the praises and features of how each was revolutionary; it was only at the end of the unveiling that the audience realized that all three products were actually combined into one - the iPhone.

This strategy has been a staple for Steve Jobs over the years, focusing on three key points. Be it at a sales meeting, with his product design and engineer teams, a product unveiling, or his famous Stanford commencement speech. Anytime he wanted to captivate his audience and have them remember key points, he would always use the "Rule of Three."

What does Steve Jobs know about the Rule of Three?

Having studied human psychology, Jobs came across a famous study by scientist George Miller that cemented his case. Starting on Page 51 of *The Presentation Secrets of Steve Jobs* by Carmine Gallo, I've quoted some snippets: "The human mind can only hold small amounts of information... In 1956, Bell Lab's research scientist George Miller published a classic paper titled "The Magical Number Seven, Plus or Minus Two." Miller's studies showed that the human mind had a hard time retaining more than seven to nine digits.

It was a groundbreaking study at its time. And he only dealt with numbers, so expanding on Miller's research, other psychologists delved further into the human mind and our ability to retain information. Continuing:

Contemporary scientists have put the number of items we can easily recall closer to three or four. So, it should not be surprising that Jobs rarely offers more than three [or four] key message points. As for that, in a Steve Jobs presentation, the number three is much more common than four. Steve understands that the "Rule of Three" is one of the most POWERFUL CONCEPTS in communication theory.

Three is that magic number.

Think about this for a second: when speeches, plays, TV shows, stories, or just about anything is grouped in threes, the human mind has a much higher likelihood of retaining and recalling the three aspects that the storyteller is trying to convey.

This is the reason that Goldilocks discovered the *Three Bears*, not four, eating her porridge. The same reason there was the story of the "Three Little Pigs," not the four little pigs. There were the Three Musketeers and the Three Stooges. The grouping of three is more impactful than two. And at three, you are less likely to forget a point as you would if there were four or five. The "Rule of Three" is also why theatrical plays are typically broken into three acts. And most great movies and books have this same three-act structure.

Furthermore, our Founding Fathers knew of The Principal of the Rule of Three, as the Declaration of Independence says that Americans have the rights of "Life, Liberty, and the pursuit of Happiness."

Gallo gives another great example:

The U.S. Marine Corps has conducted extensive research into this subject and has concluded that three is more effective than two or four. Divisions within the marines are divided into three: a corporal commands a team of three; a sergeant commands three rifle teams in a squad; a captain has three platoons and so on.

Steve Jobs knew this. He Studied it. He Perfected it.

It's also why at IMPACT we research human psychology. We are always trying to find little-known nuggets that could help home sellers gain an advantage when selling their homes. "The Rule of Three" is one of the most powerful tools any storyteller can use to increase retention.

"The Rule of Three" is an amazing strategy to get your point across and, more importantly, not to clutter your viewer/listener/reader with too many facts that overwhelm them to the point that they don't remember anything that you are trying to convey.

When you desire to get your audience to remember what you are presenting, sticking with the basic premise of the "Rule of Three" increases your chances exponentially.

How can the "Rule of Three" be applied to selling your home?

Far too often, I've seen that home sellers and the agents selling those homes will try to focus on every little detail of the house. They do this because they don't want to "leave anything out."

This a flawed strategy and one that can lead to unnecessary costs and lost profits when trying to spell out every little detail. "The fourth bedroom has plush crème carpet" (as an example). While agents think they are helping their client by listing every little detail about the home, they are actually doing a disservice. The agent is overloading the prospective buyer with TOO MUCH information and since the human brain can only retain three pieces of information about your home, if your ad has 25 features listed, which three are buyers going to remember?

Who knows, it might be the three most unimportant features and could actually be a deterrent.

One of our agents was recently on an appointment with a prospective seller who had been unsuccessful in selling their home. They found one of our listings, read our property stories and sought us out for advice on selling their home. They recognized the fact that stories sell, but they DID NOT understand the "Rule of Three."

An IMPACT agent went to meet with them on a Saturday morning and quickly realized that they would not be a good fit. How did he know?

Three reasons: First, they wanted to share every little detail about their home. The wife spent 45 minutes describing how the stones around their pool were hand-picked from some quarry and that this one particular stone, when the light struck it just right, looked like a diamond. When the agent tried to explain to them that they shouldn't overload the potential buyers with too much information, this went right over her head. So, she started to explain about the skimmer covers on her pool. She just DIDN'T GET IT!

You simply CANNOT overload buyers with every minor detail, as this clutters their thinking. The last thing you want them remembering when they get home are those darn stones and not your gorgeous wood floors.

Second, these sellers had unrealistic expectations on how the IMPACT process worked. They wanted to dictate the sales process and the showings. **This is not how we teach our sellers to gain the highest profits.** If sellers are not going to be flexible with showings and allowing buyers into their home, this is a MAJOR hurdle that can rarely be overcome.

Third, they questioned every step of preparing their home for sale. The agent explained that to present their home in the best light, A, B, and C had to be completed. Their response was, "Well, we don't agree with that."

So, what did our agent do? He told them right at that time, "Thank you for meeting with me today. I don't think that you'll be a good fit for my approach and philosophies." They were flabbergasted. A real estate agent turning down a client?

But see, when you have principles and steps to success in helping clients, when you have proven success stories of clients and how you have extracted hidden profits. When you know how to best present a home, but the sellers won't take the suggestions, then it is best not to even start that relationship.

I bring up this example because at the core, these sellers did not understand the psychology of selling a home.

When sellers try to focus on THEMSELVES (and not the potential purchaser) it is a formula for disaster. They will go through multiple real estate agents, will have price reduction after price reduction, and will have a bitter taste in their mouths about selling their home because they don't understand that what one person *likes* can and will turn someone else completely off. And they wanted TOO much information about their home to be featured, instead of focusing on its three major selling points.

Conversely, when sellers DO understand the psychology, like Bob and Sue M., whose home we sold for $12,000 over other comparable properties in the neighborhood, you get feedback like this:

> "The entire process, from first contact through closing, was completed flawlessly. My wife and I established a strong partnership with [our agent] that was instrumental in the success of the sale of our home. The process is fresh and, in my opinion, works!"

Bob and Sue, unlike the other couple, GOT IT. They understood the psychology of buyers and they understood the "Rule of Three." We wrote their story by focusing on three things: room sizes, an updated kitchen, and a large, level yard. We went into detail and told a beautiful story about their home, but we didn't clutter the reader—the potential buyer—with mundane extras.

That is why, when using the strategies of Steve Jobs and "The Psychological Approach to Sell Real Estate," we take a page directly out of Jobs' playbook. Your home's story is carefully constructed, keeping the "Rule of Three" in mind.

There are three MAIN benefits of your home that need to be told in its story. Under each of the three main points, there may be other minor feature points that reiterate the main points.

By keeping your story simple and by following the "Rule of Three," we can focus on the features of your home that we want the buyer to notice! Eliminate the clutter.

Eliminate the noise. Don't overload the buyer.

If Steve Jobs were to come to your house to help you sell, he would follow this exact formula. He was able to take Apple from the brink of bankruptcy to being the most valuable company in the world, based around this "Rule of Three" strategy.

If it worked for Apple, it'll work for you!

CHAPTER SIX

FUNDAMENTAL STRATEGY #3

Don't Invent, Innovate

The day before something is a breakthrough, it's a crazy idea." — Peter Diamandis, founder of the XPrize

D id Facebook invent social media? Did Amazon invent book sales or selling products online? No, the path was already laid. The inventions happened prior to the enormous success of these companies.

The INNOVATION happened when they found better uses for these prior inventions.

They adapted the core concepts, molded with other industries, and BAM! A new innovation that society and consumers devoured was born, and we wondered, "How did we ever do without that?"

In a recent article in the *Washingtonian*, "Steve Jobs was a Businessman, Not an Artist," the following passage compares Henry Ford to Steve Jobs:

> Ford did not invent the car, just as Jobs did not invent the computer. He popularized the car, taking an invention that was, until then, for the elite, and democratizing it. He did

this not just by making it affordable to the middle class; he also sold the public on the idea that his cars were essential to their lives.

Jobs had a famous quote that he happily recited numerous times when people accused him of "stealing" others' inventions. It was a quote originally from Pablo Picasso: "Good artists copy; great artists steal."

Jobs, of course, didn't steal others' ideas, or he would have had patent and copyright lawsuits. But what he was able to do and what was one of his greatest strengths was innovation.

The Definition of "Innovation" from *Business Dictionary* **is** "the deliberate application of information, imagination, and initiative in deriving greater or DIFFERENT values from resources…converting into useful products."

Jobs was able to see opportunity where others couldn't.

There are dozens of times throughout his career when he was able to use innovation of existing products and transform them for the betterment of Apple.

Here are three examples of how geniuses like Jobs used innovation to propel them down their path toward success.

1. **The Renegade Space Race**

Founder of the XPrize Foundation, Peter Diamandis, was always passionate about the impossible: making things no one believed could happen come to life.

After watching the Apollo 11 moon landing in July 1969, Diamandis was determined to fly into space himself. So, he completed two degrees from MIT and a medical degree from Harvard; he had put himself in a prime position for acceptance into NASA's Astronaut Corps - where he could be trained to join U.S. astronauts on international space missions.

But soon he realized the traditional path was not going to get him where he needed to go. NASA was winding down their space program, and they simply didn't share his vision.

So Diamandis went back to the drawing board. He learned about a 1920's entrepreneur, a French hotelier named Raymond Orteig, who offered up a $25,000 prize to the first person who could fly nonstop from New York to Paris during the golden age of aviation.

You know who won the prize? Charles Lindbergh - the same man who set into motion the creation of today's commercial airline industry. In other words, Southwest Airlines and "TransFAREncy" would not be what it is today without Orteig and Lindbergh.

It also wouldn't be what it is today without innovation. Neither would SpaceX or Diamandis.

In 1996, Diamandis unveiled a $10 million prize for the first nongovernment team who could successfully fly a manned rocket to space - in under two weeks.

Before long, 24 teams from over a dozen countries were competing. In 2004, American aerospace engineer Burt Rutan won the prize with his original design of the first privately created suborbital spaceplane, SpaceShipOne.

Now, world-famous entrepreneurs Richard Branson and Elon Musk have joined Diamandis and are working together to create the world's first private space program.

Diamandis had two choices when the traditional path failed him: give up or innovate. Thankfully, he chose innovation.

2. The iBOT

You might not know the name Dean Kamen, but chances are you *have* heard of (and have probably seen) his signature invention, the Segway. The two-wheeled motorized vehicle came out right after the 9/11 attacks and because of that gained instant fame and recognition. It was a welcome change and created a pop culture kind of excitement right away.

But if you ask Kamen, the Segway is neither his biggest money-maker n*or* his best invention. Kamen strives to use innovation to improve the lives of others.

He did just that with his self-balancing, battery-powered, multi-terrain wheelchair (the iBOT), which was launched in 1992, allowing disabled people to do the same things non-disabled people do in public, like going up a curb or standing eye level to the person they are talking to.

Kamen got the idea for the iBOT after watching a man at a mall struggling to pay for an ice cream cone when he couldn't reach the counter. What Kamen realized was that the problem was not the wheelchair at all - the problem was that the world was designed for people who could "self-balance." So, all he needed to do was create a chair that provided a balancing feature. So, he teamed up with Johnson & Johnson to create the Independent iBOT Mobility System - a chair that has the ability to climb stairs and cruise right over rocks, sand and curbs.

iBOT solves these mobility issues by giving the person using the chair the ability to self-balance.

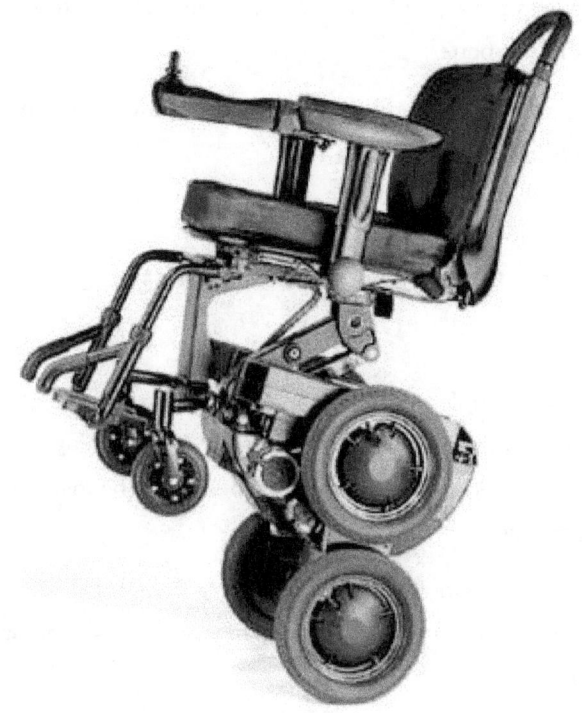

Kamen is the true definition of someone who is *always innovating*.

Right now, he has over 400 U.S. patents, has created things like the modern insulin pump, robotic prosthetic limbs and a water purification device called the "Slingshot" and even has his own island off the coast of Connecticut, which he uses as his own high-tech headquarters.

Dean and 500 engineers and technicians from his company, DEKA Research, are working right now on some of the most forward-thinking tools to help people in the third world gain access to cleaner drinking water and gain an overall better quality of life.

Needless to say, he is a perfect example of how innovation makes our lives better.

"Science and technology and engineering and innovating, it's for everybody," says Kamen.

3. From Corningware to "Gorilla Glass"

The last example of innovation comes from the time Apple was just getting ready to unveil the iPhone. Jobs was involved at every turn and decided that the screen needed to be made of a superior product.

The excerpt below, from *The Man Who Thought Different* by Karen Blumenthal, explains this story best and reveals the origins of "Gorilla Glass."

> *"He decided that the elegant screen had to be glass (not plastic) since plastic was too likely to scratch. Glass could scratch, too, and it breaks. So, Jobs had to find a material that was unusually strong. His search led him to Corning Incorporated... In 1962, Corning developed "muscled glass" that was used in cars and planes, but it was discontinued in the early 1990s.*

When Jobs heard about the material, he asked for everything Corning could make in the next six months. That seemed impossible, since nothing was being made at all. But Jobs insisted. "Get your mind around it. You can do it," Jobs told Wendell Weeks, Corning's chief executive.

Within six months, Corning had dusted off its old formula, improved on it, and started up production at a Kentucky factory. The new material, named "Gorilla Glass," covered the iPhone and eventually hundreds of other consumer gadgets with a remarkably tough glass."

Where others, even inventors of this amazing product, saw failure and obsolescence, Jobs saw an opportunity. Apple didn't invent "Gorilla Glass" or even the concept, but Jobs made Corning *innovate* and repurpose a prior product with amazing success.

"Innovation distinguishes between a leader and a follower." – Steve Jobs

When looking for ways to help our clients, we are always looking at other industries to see what is working that we can adapt to help our sellers achieve hidden profits on their home sale. If we were to only look inside the real estate industry, then we would just be giving our clients a tired retread that someone else used. We would NOT be innovating.

That's why at IMPACT we study some of the best of all time: Joseph Sugarman, Dan Kennedy, David Ogilvy, Jay Abraham, Eugene Schwartz, and Gary Halbert, to name a few. (If you are unfamiliar with these names, Google them, and you will see hundreds of books written by and about these people.) We are fascinated with how they could sell hundreds of millions of dollars of product through the written word.

Through our research, we also realized that we could create property stories for the listings (as you recall from Fundamental Strategy #1 – Story-Selling) that would help create an emotional attachment for potential purchasers. We also found that the more ways you can convey the message (i.e. the story) of the house to purchasers, the higher the likelihood that your home will stand out against the competition and create value to the purchaser.

Annie, our photographer, always does an amazing job presenting the property's story via photos, and buyers often comment that "it was the pictures that drew us in; that they were the reason we wanted to see the home." Annie depicts a visual story and representation of each home.

However, some people can better retain information from reading a story and visualizing. They prefer to create an image of the home in their own mind.

If we only did a visual story with each home, we'd be cutting out the people who retain written information better and form their own visualization.

For that reason, we have adapted what has worked in other industries, direct response sales, novels, and books and molded into our written property stories. Once a potential buyer reads one of our stories, they have an emotional attachment to the home, and buyers purchase on emotion.

Property Stories, like "Gorilla Glass" being dusted off by Jobs from Corning is certainly not new. But when it comes to putting words on paper, to write a story that hits on the reader's emotions, that is one of the *key innovations* that has helped our sellers consistently achieve record-breaking profits.

Innovation is the Key

Like Jobs with Apple, we are always asking ourselves: *How can we look to other industries to find new kinds of innovation that we can mold them to fit our industry and benefit our clients?*

Sometimes, asking ourselves that question has led to iPhone type breakthroughs for the real estate world - breakthroughs like Scientifically Staging homes in a way that earns our clients $40,000 in profits. It has also led to breakthroughs like bringing in a top-of-the-line photographer who weaves a beautiful story for the buyer with every shot.

Other times, we make mini breakthroughs, like when Apple increased the megapixels of the iPhone. We craft property stories that help potential buyers form an instant bond with the home and buy into the story so much that they couldn't see themselves anywhere else. We use the "Rule of Three" and find the key features in every home we sell that communicate the true value it holds.

Think about it this way: Jobs was able to look at Xerox and know before anyone else that they "were sitting on a gold mine."

Their idea was ahead of its time, and he wasn't afraid to innovate and adapt the product for the betterment of the consumers of his Apple product.

The same way, we are always looking at methods used outside of the real estate industry that will bring benefit and value to our customers.

If you aren't innovating in real estate, or any industry for that matter, you will always be chasing, not leading. At IMPACT, we follow the path of Diamandis, Kane and Jobs.

We are always innovating. And because of that, we are always creating a better sales reality for our clients.

CHAPTER SEVEN

FUNDAMENTAL STRATEGY #4

Hero vs. Villain

The Contrast Principle

"We're a product company. We love great products. In order to explain what our product is, we have to contrast it to what products are out there right now and what people use." — Steve Jobs

First, take the above quote. Then, replace the word "product" with "home," and you have a strategy for success.

Your home must contrast with everything else on the market right now, or you <u>will</u> be lost in a sea of online searches. How do you do this? By using the Contrast Principle, which I'll explain later in this chapter.

Following the Contrast Principle could mean the difference between selling your home and having it sit on the market for months until you have lost $30,000-$40,000 in profits and months of sleepless nights.

Remember the hilarious television ads that ran from 2006 to 2009 that featured two guys? One guy was a young, cool dude in casual clothing, and the other was a dorky-looking guy, slightly overweight, and with glasses. They would talk about each of their features.

The "cool" guy would talk about what he could do, how user-friendly he was, how he never got "bogged" down. The "dorky" guy would try to counteract each of the cool guy's points but would fail miserably. Each guy represented a company. The cool guy was a smaller underdog taking on the big corporate giant—the dorky guy.

Who was the brainchild behind this ad campaign that featured Mac vs. PC? That's right, Apple - which was run by Steve Jobs.

See, what Jobs knows is that every good story has a hero and a villain.

Good versus Evil. The classic Antagonist vs. Protagonist. First, you introduce the Antagonist (the problem). Then, you unite the audience around the Hero. This is exactly what Jobs did with the famous Mac vs. PC ad campaign that was a smashing success and even evolved into getting endorsements from famous people, who publicly said they were Mac users. The genius behind this campaign was that it "rallied" the audience around the Hero (Apple/Mac) against the big, evil giant (PC).

The same formula is used all the time in novels, TV shows, corporate branding strategies, comic books, and movies. What would Batman do if there was no Joker? How about Coke vs. Pepsi? Nike vs. Reebok? Verizon vs. Sprint? Avis vs. Hertz? FedEx vs. USPS? When competing for the same dollar from consumers, you need to build your brand and gain a rabid, loyal following. The best way to do this is to have a villain with whom you are competing.

Presenting the Hero vs. Villain strategy correctly can have immediate and long-lasting benefits when introducing products.

You introduce the villain. Talk about the villain's features. Then, solve the problem that the villain causes by introducing the hero.

Another example of Jobs' brilliant use of this Hero vs. Villain scenario was when he introduced the iPhone. [Jobs made the following points, and others, during his unveiling.] Before the iPhone revolutionized "smartphones," the state-of-the-art phones at that time (Blackberry, Palm Treo, etc.) all had these awkward keyboards. Their user interface was tough to navigate. They had 40 buttons, and you had no idea what half of them did. Some had a stylus that you would either lose or break. (Trust me, I went through a number of them.)

Jobs built up the "Villain" as an outdated, slow, awkward phone with limited capabilities. Then, with each point, he would introduce a new, modern, sleeker, more efficient solution to the problem. Each solution built upon the last until he introduced the iPhone. Enter the "Protagonist."

If you remember, the iPhone was the breakthrough smartphone that changed the industry. Gone were the awkward keypads. Gone was the exterior keyboard of the phone. In came the full-size screen. Gone were the unnecessary buttons and flimsy stylus. All of a sudden, you could use your finger (a man-made stylus). The iPhone had the capability to hold music, so you no longer had to have two devices for communication and music. Plus, the browsing (internet) options on the iPhone were also revolutionary.

Jobs knew exactly what he wanted to do and how he wanted to position the iPhone. Thus, he was wildly successful in differentiating Apple products from the competitors' products.

Think of your home as "The Hero."

Subconsciously, when purchasers are looking at homes, they fall back into the habit of comparing one home to the next. In his book, *Influence: The Psychology of Persuasion,* Dr. Robert Cialdini refers to this as the Contrast Principle. In the field of psychophysics, the contrast principle is well-established and common knowledge. There is a principle in human perception that affects the way we see differences between objects, and if the second object is vastly different than the first, then the "perception" of the difference between the two objects is magnified.

In one experiment (which you can do at home) you start with three buckets of water: one ice-cold; the other, hot; and the third at room temperature. Then, you stick your hands in the hot and cold water, individually, yet at the same time. Then, put *both* of your hands in the room temperature bucket. Even though that water is the same temperature, the hand that was in the cold bucket now feels hot, and vice-versa. This is an example the contrast principle using your sense of touch.

The *Contrast Principle* can also be just as powerful visually.

Make your house "stand-out" against the competition (the Villains) so that when a potential buyer sees your home, their "perception" is so different than everything else they've seen that they MUST buy your home.

Have you ever received an Apple product? The presentation is simple, yet sophisticated, and you feel like you are unwrapping the future.

When unveiling your home to potential buyers, you want to accomplish the same thing. Make them feel as if they are unwrapping their future - their new home. Take specific steps to make sure buyers see your home in a positive light compared to the competition—the other homes they could purchase instead of yours.

There are two ways to make sure that your home is presented correctly to the potential buyers through what is called the Continuity Principle. The first is visually. Your home's photos must POP, must entice buyers to drop what they are doing and call to schedule a showing of your home. The second is through the written word. A properly written "story" can create an emotional attachment to your home. Once the buyer is emotionally invested, their obstacles to making an offer are eliminated.

Humans learn and retain information differently.

Some are visual retainers; some retain better with written words. This is why it is important to not only have your photos POP, but to also have a unique, descriptive, emotionally-enhanced story written about your home.

A study by Dr. Richard Mayer of the University of California concluded that when combining words and pictures, the retention rate was 65% better than having just one or the other. Mayer says, "The Continuity Principle is not surprising if you know how the brain works."

"When the brain is allowed to build <u>two</u> mental representations...the mental connections are that much stronger."

Your home's story is not only visually told through amazing photos, but also with a corresponding property story that is written to create an emotional attachment. One without the other eliminates half of the population, because everyone retains information differently.

Recently at IMPACT, we had two sellers, Bill and Gina, who wanted to test the upper limits of the market. They wanted to try and price their home for $20,000 over what everything else in the area was selling.

We knew these sellers would follow *every* piece of advice we gave them, so we gave them a shot without giving them any promises about the outcome. We explained to them that IF there was any chance of getting the target price, then we would have to do A, B, and C.

They did exactly what was outlined by the stagers, and when we took the pictures, the home photographed amazingly. These were some of the best pictures that I've ever seen and were definitely magazine-worthy. On top of that, the sellers kept the house as clean as a whistle. We even joked with them every time we went over: "Are you sure that you are still living here?"

Their home was clear of clutter; the kitchen was always spotless. The bathrooms were perfect; the hardwood was clean, and the carpet was vacuumed. It was Leonardo da Vinci who said, "Simplicity is the ultimate sophistication."

We wrote their home's story in a four-page article format (which could have also been in a magazine). All of our bases were covered, and their home was well-delivered to the market, both visually and through written word.

After two weeks and 12 showings, the house STOOD OUT from the competition, and people fell in love with the home.

Within three weeks, we had two offers, one of which we accepted. A week later, we received a backup offer from someone else who just "had to have it." The contract price shattered every other home sale in the area because of the presentation and the fact that, when compared to every other home in the immediate area, their home blew away the competition.

Bill and Gina had this to say:

- "[IMPACT] listened and provided guidance in a comforting, professional, knowledgeable way. [They] really held our hands through the entire process of selling our home and went above and beyond our expectations."

This example demonstrates the power of the Contrast Principle and how, when selling your home, it is import to differentiate it from the competition.

Much like the Mac vs. PC ad in the late 2000s, your home sale should be viewed as the Hero (your home) versus the Villain (your competition). Make sure you are the Hero, *not the Villain*, by using the strategies outlined throughout this book.

CHAPTER EIGHT

FUNDAMENTAL STRATEGY #5

The Power of TEAM

"Teamwork is the ability to work together toward a common vision. The ability to direct individual accomplishments toward organizational objectives. It is the fuel that allows common people to attain uncommon results." -- Andrew Carnegie

Henry Ford did not invent the assembly line. He didn't invent the gasoline engine. He didn't invent the automobile. In fact, Ford didn't invent much of anything at all.

Yet, by 1947, the Ford Motor Company had forged a deep impact on the world. In just four decades, Ford had (as he put it) "invented the modern age." How did he accomplish so much in such little time?

Ford had a dream for, about and with the "everyman." He also knew how all the "moving parts" of a man-made team would come together to make the dream a reality.

His vision was to make a car that was "affordable for the masses." But his true skill was in how he would use "mass talent" to get there.

Before 1903 and the beginning of the Ford Motor Company, Ford knew he could build a car. He was already a successful racer and racing car manufacturer. But he also knew he couldn't build a car fast enough to sell it in bulk.

After setting up his first shop and hiring his first crew of workers, Ford and his men had successfully created 500 Model A's. He sold them to doctors and lawyers and made a pretty good profit, but his dream was far from realized.

The next challenge? To create a car that was affordable enough for the average "Joe" to buy. In just a few years, he created the Model T (or "Tin Lizzie"). It was simpler, reliable and cheaper than anything else on the market. In fact, within just a few months, Ford got so many orders for the Model T that he had to stop sales. They simply couldn't keep up with demand.

Even most visionaries in Ford's shoes would have had trouble getting past this kind of obstacle. Ford didn't have a creative problem now. He had a 'people' problem.

How was he going to rally his team quickly enough to meet this new demand?

That's when today's modern assembly line was born. Ford wondered if he could yield the power of his people better when they're focused on doing one thing and doing it really well. If he adapted the production process around his people (rather than the other way around) he could skyrocket his output and cut production time in half. Turns out he was right!

After dragging a chassis by rope and a windlass across the floor of his Highland Park plant, his theory was tested and proved correct. In under a year, Ford and his team were producing a new car every 93 minutes!

True vision is about looking around you to see what resources are at your disposal. For Ford, the greatest resource he had was his TEAM.

When his team became fatigued by the repetitive nature of the assembly line, Ford again saw an opportunity to boost his team's morale. He raised their wages to $5 per day (nearly twice the going rate). Morale and production improved drastically.

Don't get me wrong here. Ford was no perfect leader. He has faced his fair share of criticism over the years for his leadership style, which went through a lot of changes through the years (especially during the Depression).

However, at every turn, Ford was willing and able to make the changes he needed to make to propel his team forward and give them the motivation they need to excel.

Great entrepreneurs innovate. However, great leaders innovate in a way that inspires their TEAM to innovate, perform and succeed in their own right.

In business, like sports, companies take on the characteristics of the CEO/President/Leader.

It doesn't matter if it is a huge international company like Apple, Southwest, or Amazon or a smaller local company; the team/employees follows the lead and direction of their "leader."

Believe it or not, Steve Jobs built Apple in the hopes of gaining some wisdom on human psychology, yet he turned it into an international powerhouse with loyal customers. Apple, at its core (no pun intended), was built on the backbone and vision of Steve Jobs, along with the seven core psychological principles.

Here, we found nuggets of wisdom that we could bring to the real estate business.

Steve Jobs was the visionary, the leader, the CEO of Apple, and he set the course and direction. Steve Jobs was so successful that he built Apple not once, with Apple II and Mac, but twice. After he was ousted from his position as CEO by the board of directors, Apple lost Jobs' vision. Consequently, they also lost their way.

Apple's board of directors realized they made a HUGE mistake by firing Jobs, and he was rehired. It was during this second tenure that Apple revolutionized the music industry and forever changed how we listen to music with the iPod. Then later, with Jobs' vision, Apple released the iPad and iPhone.

What most don't know is that Apple's innovations were not Jobs' direct inventions; they were either adapted from other industries or improved upon. It was Jobs' vision that led Apple through both boom periods. Jobs was not an expert programmer. Although he knew coding and how to build software, Jobs was not this great "inventor." Apple, under Jobs' leadership, had a TEAM of expert programmers.

Every company had expert programmers, but what made Apple different started with Jobs and his vision. Unlike other companies, Jobs fostered innovations; he encouraged his team to think outside of the box and to always look for ways to improve! Yes, Jobs was a great marketer, an expert presenter, and even gave the commencement speech to the Stanford graduating class of 2005.

Steve Jobs' greatest asset was being a leader and creating a movement.

The "Think Different" campaign came from Jobs. This was Apple's motto, and the ad campaign behind it was hugely successful. Jobs was the captain of the ship and, through his stewardship, led a revolution that spanned from the 1970s to today.

At IMPACT, we have a TEAM of Professionals who go together to every listing.

First, we have our core team we bring to every property. We also have other professionals we partner with to enhance the value of your home. We have painters, landscapers, siding professionals, carpet and hardwood professionals, contacts with manufactures and roofers. Anyone that you need to help properly present your home for sale is in our 'Rolodex.' Leave the coordinating to the professionals.

We also bring in stagers to "Scientifically Stage" the home. Our stagers are the best at what they do and can make a lived-in home look as close to a model home as possible. Equally important is that they work hand-in-hand with Annie Main, who photographs a home better than anyone we've ever seen.

Our stagers know the angle from which Annie will take the photos. So, they can focus their attention on each room individually, based on how Annie will photograph them. This way, each room and each photo tells an individual story.

Consider your home's story as a book, with each room being a chapter. It is our team's job to make sure each chapter fits the overall theme of the book.

We understand firsthand that if one chapter of the book does not flow with the others, the "story" will be lost upon the reader. Or, in this case, the buyer.

Having an incomplete or confusing story could cost a seller tens of thousands of dollars.

Our job is to find hidden ways to extract additional profits for sellers. To that end, we have been able to construct five stories that have allowed the sellers to achieve the five highest sales per square foot in their respective neighborhoods since 2014. Like Henry Ford did with his Model T and V8 engine, and as Steve Jobs did in building Apple twice, when you surround yourself with an outstanding team, provide direction, and lead that team, amazing results can happen.

The results achieved by Ford and Jobs were not luck or happenstance; they were the result of providing the vision, hiring the right team, and letting the team achieve the vision.

Our clients say it best when referring to our TEAM:

> -Having relocated out of the area before listing my home, I needed not only a great real estate agent but also someone I could trust to take care of all of the processes involved in selling a home with only being able to get back to the area on a sporadic basis. Shortly after I listed the home with him, it sold after four days on the market. The whole process went flawlessly... [IMPACT's] TEAM did a fantastic job on staging the home, marketing, pricing,

necessary inspections, and coordination with the buyer's agent. - Jeff B.

- [IMPACT] was an excellent TEAM of professionals who made the overall process super smooth, from photography to repairs. And they do the job right! – Dennis and Jennifer W.

In business, there is not a clear-cut winner and loser. There are only the lessons that we learn, and what we do with those lessons to better ourselves and those around us that can help us innovate breakthroughs.

CHAPTER NINE

FUNDAMENTAL STRATEGY #6

Creating a Buzz

"Orchestrating Buzz—Following the Hollywood Script."

The smartest companies in the world understand basic economics and the law of supply and demand. But, more importantly, they understand how to create a buzz and excitement for their product before it even hits the market.

Steve Jobs was a master Marketer, a master Innovator, and an incredible Storyteller. But without being able to manufacture a buzz amongst consumers, his other skills would have gone unnoticed. Jobs knew how to release a product, how to promote certain aspects of the product while leaving other details to the imagination of the public. He knew the best time to release a product and how to engineer demand to a fever pitch, right up to the release date.

This led to an unprecedented buzz for any new product that Apple introduced. The only industry that could match his marketing and buzz is the movie industry. That's why Apple had a cult-like following every fall in anticipation of Apple's latest gadget. Consumers would sleep outside of the Apple Store for hours—days, even—waiting for their latest product to be unveiled. This was a culture that Steve Jobs was able to form with Apple.

What if the same strategies that Steve Jobs and many other master marketers used to create a buzz for their products could be used for your home sale?

What if you could have people—consumers and purchasers—anticipating your home coming onto the market, seeing your home online, looking at the photos, reading the property story, and calling or texting their agent in the middle of the night, saying, "I need to see this house tomorrow. If the house looks like the photos, I've got to buy it."

That is the buzz that I'm talking about. Remember the story from the "Why This Book?" chapter? The story about the female doctor who sent her husband to see the home and told him that if it looks anything like the photos, he should submit the offer? Yes, that is the power of creating demand and a buzz through properly positioning a home for sale.

Much like the movie industry and Hollywood, if the marketing is done correctly with a strategically-induced buzz, the first three weeks on the market is the optimal time to get a contract for maximum value.

Think about it for a minute.

Why does Hollywood spend millions upon millions of dollars promoting a movie for four weeks, six weeks, or two months in anticipation of the release date? What do they know that you don't? They know that 90% of their sales are going to occur in the first two to three weekends on the market, and that over 50% of their sales will be during the first three days on the market. Why do they release movies when they do? What is the timing of it? What day of the week?

It's the same way we release your house to the market. There are reasons why we take the photos on the day that we take them, and why your home hits social media at a certain time. And, like a movie release, your list date is anticipated weeks (if not months) in advance—all planned to create a BUZZ and, ultimately, maximize the value of your home.

Back to Economics 101. The *supply* is your house against other competing homes on the market. The *demand* is the buzz—the excitement that we can generate from listing your house properly and properly presenting it to the market.

Once consumers see your house online, we want them to say, "I must see that house. I *must* see that house."

This can be done correctly, or it can be done like most real estate agents do—poorly. They haphazardly list houses. They don't have set schedules of release dates, and they don't know how to properly engineer a BUZZ.

With these kinds of agents, the pictures aren't in any particular order. Photos aren't professionally done. The tours are inadequate, at best. The videos—yeah, you'll see them on YouTube, and they'll be shot with an iPhone. (Note: iPhones are capable of capturing good videos of your kids playing in the backyard.) However, if you are trying to sell your home, would you rather it be shot on an iPhone or with a professional videographer who can capture *every* essence of your home?

Alternatively, your photos could be strategically aligned for maximum exposure in the market.

See exhibits 6.1 through 6.3 as examples of the kind of buzz that can be engineered if done properly. Over half of the total page views you see happening here occur within the first weekend on the market. *80% are within the first week.* This is why I say that, like a Hollywood movie, your best chance of obtaining an offer is within the first three weeks, but really the first week on the market. The buzz will dictate the end result and whether you, the seller, are walking away with record-breaking sales or months on the market with multiple price drops and tens of thousands of dollars lost.

Just like Apple, Steve Jobs and the Hollywood filmmakers create buzz around their products - if the buzz and the excitement around your house's entering the market is done properly, it can capture the essence and the emotion of a purchaser.

Once the emotion is there, wonderful, record-breaking offers aren't far behind.

Exhibit 6.1

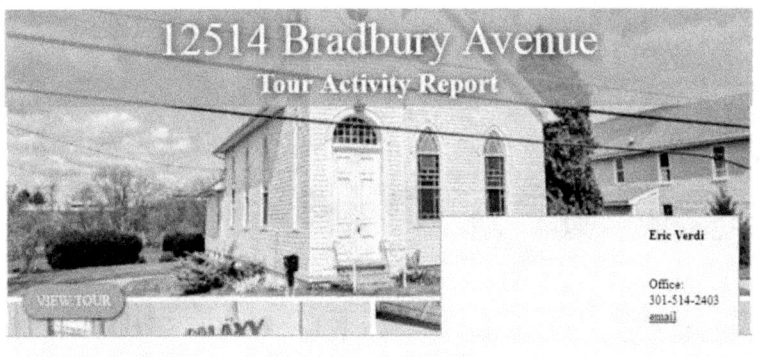

164,856 6,283 5,719 28.8

Total photos viewed | Total tour views | Total visitors | Images viewed per visitor

Popular Images

#1 7,917 views | #2 7,441 views | #3 6,843 views | #4 6,558 views

#5 6,308 views | #6 6,142 views | #7 6,008 views | #8 5,989 views

#9 5,878 views | #10 5,819 views | #11 5,747 views | #12 5,737 views

Exhibit 6.2

44,217
Total photos viewed

1,354
Total tour views

1,204
Total visitors

36.7
Images viewed per visitor

Popular Images

#1 1,668 views   #2 1,546 views   #3 1,416 views   #4 1,372 views

#5 1,305 views   #6 1,270 views   #7 1,239 views   #8 1,217 views

#9 1,186 views   #10 1,142 views   #11 1,136 views   #12 1,117 views

Exhibit 6.3

5318 Henden Wood Lane
Tour Activity Report

34,042
Total photos viewed

1,044
Total tour views

893
Total visitors

38.1
Images viewed per visitor

Popular Images

#1 1,295 views #2 1,190 views #3 1,154 views #4 1,152 views

#5 1,104 views #6 1,075 views #7 1,063 views #8 1,055 views

#9 1,003 views #10 966 views #11 940 views #12 911 views

CHAPTER TEN

FUNDAMENTAL STRATEGY #7

Correct Timing Eliminates Uncertainty

"Observe due measure, for right timing is in all things the most Important factor." - Hesiod

Anyone who has made any kind of investment in the market (whether that investment was in stocks, bonds or REITs) can tell you that following the "buy low, sell high" Value-Driven Approach to investing is not as easy as it looks.

Let's say you get a windfall of money - an inheritance from your grandmother or a big chunk of gains from a recent investment. You go to an advisor who says, "Invest it now." They tell you the market is surging right now, so you need to get the stocks before they go too high! (Plus, we know they are ready to get the high commission).

But you hear from your conservative investor friend down the street who says that Wall Street analysts predict a market dip further down the road. The market cannot sustain itself for long, he says, and the market will adjust itself. You just wait and see. Your time to invest will come.

Six months later, you're wishing you didn't follow the advice of the analysts. You're watching stock returns tick up, up and up. You're slapping yourself for not getting in when you could, and you're itching to play your hand and make as much as you can before it's too late.

Two months after you've dealt your cards and put your money in, the market takes the dive the analysts predicted all along. Game over. Thousands have made the same timing miscalculation, and for that reason, their returns are going down.

Playing the 'timing' game in the world of investing is not for the faint of heart.

No one thinks they're going to be an emotional investor. Everyone thinks they'll be logical, steady and follow the advice of Buffett and every other seasoned investor who says "Buy low, sell high." It's the investment timing equivalent of your Kindergarten ABC's.

But it is hard to follow. *Why?* Because we can't see the future. We can only see what's right in front of us.

And the only way we're going to listen to timing advice that goes against what we're seeing with our own two eyes is if it comes from a trusted source - someone who we know for sure has found success with their own timing instincts.

Someone like Warren Buffett, who made $53,000 by the time he was 16, just by playing the market and investing his cash as the right time for ultimate gains.

In 1988, Buffett invested $108 million in Freddie Mac, a government-backed mortgage insurance firm. At the time, shares were selling for just $4 a piece. Ten years, later, each share was worth $70 and Buffett was still fully vested. That was until he had a meeting with Freddie Mac's CEO, Leland Brendsel in 2000. During the meeting, Buffett picked up some leadership decisions that were concerning, and within a year he had dumped all his stock in the company. By 2003, Freddie Mac was making the news for regularly misreporting its earnings. By 2008, during the financial crisis, the company was being bailed out by the government and shares reached an all-time low of $2.

Because he gauged the TIME right at both the beginning and the end, Buffett earned a whopping 1,525% return!

Without his sense of timing, however, his losses would have been huge.

A slight change on timing can make such a huge difference.

Now, let's relate this back to real estate and timing the market for purchasers and sellers - timing when to list your home for sale for maximum profit.

Most sellers (and agents, for that matter) seem to think that "the spring market" is the best time to sell your home. And although that might be true for some years, in other years, it is the completely wrong strategy.

For example, the winter of 2014 was one of those unusual markets. That was the winter with the massive snowfalls. It seemed as if it snowed every week. Schools were always closed. There were freezing temperatures and power outages. During that period, we also couldn't seem to keep homes on the market.

There was about a two-and-a-half-month period from the end of December through the middle of February when we couldn't keep *any* homes on the market. IMPACT listed eight homes during that period. The homes hit the market on a Thursday (there is a specific strategy and reason we do this), and on six of those homes, we had contracts accepted by the next Monday. But we had no idea why this was happening. It could have been that there was a lack of supply of homes, or may have been great interest rates. Either way, it was completely atypical to the conventional thought process on the best time is to list for maximum profits.

As this was evolving, we reached out to two clients who had been thinking about selling for at least a year.

We told them, "Guys, I'm not sure what is going on, but we can't keep listings on the market. If you are truly thinking of selling, NOW is the time."

They said yes; they both wanted to sell. So, our team sprang into action. Both homes were scientifically staged beautifully, and Annie-photographed amazingly.

The result?

First, Jeremy and Beth received an offer on their home in the first week that they were on the market. It took some time to negotiate, but the end result was that they had, and still HAVE, the highest-sold townhouse in their old neighborhood within the last five years.

Here is what they had to say about the whole experience:

- Jer and I want to send a huge shout out and thank you to our awesome realtor at [Impact Maryland Real Estate]! Through the roller-coaster ride of selling and buying, [they] were there day and night (no matter what time), to walk us through, hold our hands, and reassure us! From the beginning, [they] had our best interest at heart, from staging our home to setting up professional pictures and knowing the **perfect timing to list our home to get the maximum value!** If you're looking for a realtor that goes well above and beyond and treats you like family, then you could not ask for anyone better than [IMPACT]!

Shane and Shannon, the second couple, received two offers in the first weekend that their house was on the market. They accepted one. The kicker here was that their house hit the market during one of the huge snowstorms in 2014, and there was only one day that people could get in to see their home.

The timing of their listing allowed them to get a contract, sell, and move into a beautiful new home fast!

Timing can have as much of an impact on everything else that we do— the Scientific Staging, the professional photos, the professional cleaning, the pre-listing inspection, the written property story, the video documentary.

If the timing is right and the above are done correctly, the results can be amazing.

However, if we do everything correctly and the timing is wrong, then maximum profits may not be realized. This is one of the reasons that having a seasoned professional who monitors the local market daily and can detect trends before the public can be invaluable.

So, the next time you ask yourself, "Is now a good time to sell?" stay away from the traditional thinking and listening to the mass media.

Much like the early sale of his Freddie Mac stocks helped Buffett save his earnings, the timing of selling your home at a particular time, as compared to waiting three to four months, could put tens of thousands of additional profits in your pocket!

"The stock market is a device for transferring money from the impatient to the patient." - Warren Buffett

CHAPTER ELEVEN

WHAT'S NEXT?

"Your work is going to fill a large part of your life, and the only way to be truly satisfied is to do what you believe is great work. And the only way to do great work is to love what you do. If you haven't found it yet, keep looking. Don't settle. As with all matters of the heart, you'll know when you find it." – Steve Jobs

I f you have ever invested your hard-earned cash in a piece of electronic equipment (whether it's a tablet, laptop or iPhone) you know how hard it is when that little green light just won't turn on.

It's like a punch to the stomach. One small glitch in the system, and you're out of business. Because no matter how much money you spent on it, there is nothing you can do to bring it back to life. (That is - nothing short of going back to school to get a degree in computer engineering).

And the more you paid for that piece of equipment, the harder it is to accept.

That's why Apple created the Genius Bar.

When we have "Apple" size problems, we need "Apple" size solutions - what we DON'T need is an IT professional asking us if we turned our computer off and on. We need an expert - someone with the know-how to fill in the gaps our lack of knowledge leaves unfilled.

After all, we paid for it right?

Part of the reason people buy Apple products is because they know they are going to get 2 things: an expertly-designed product *and* expert support.

The same is true of any big-name brand out there, from coffee to hamburgers. You go to 7-Eleven to make your own coffee. You go to Starbucks to have a *barista* craft you a specialty coffee drink.

You go to a Westin hotel when you want to feel like a VIP. You stay at a Comfort Inn when you just want a night's sleep for a low price.

Even when we seek out big-name brands, it's not just the name we're chasing - it's the level of service and expertise that name brings.

That's why Apple makes its Genius Bar staff study a 60-page training manual and go through a rigorous certification process before they put on that blue shirt and sell their first "iProduct."

It's why Starbucks has TWO training programs in place for their staff. Just to get your green apron, you have to take a week-long class. Want to go to the next level and wear the sacred black apron? You need to find a sensei who will let you into the Starbucks "Coffee Master" program.

Yep, the world of luxury brand coffee is a lot like the movie Karate Kid.

But the process exists because the formula works.

Having standards for success turned Starbucks into a billion-dollar brand in less than decade.

It's the same for Apple; it's the same for Westin. And it's the same for IMPACT.

We have a core set of principles we stand by. We also know the HOW and WHY behind those principles, and our agents knows how to *use* those principles to help their clients maximize the value of their home.

But just like Starbucks, and just like Apple, there are knock-offs in the real estate profession that will tell you they can do the same.

They will offer to stage your home or take professional photos of your property. But they don't have the core principles behind them. They don't have a Documented Approach.

Selling your house to "those guys," is like staying at a Comfort Inn. It might seem like an okay idea at first, but it's a decision that will cost you at least a good night's rest.

Any agent that hands you this book, on the other hand, has gone through a rigorous training process to understand the Psychological Approach to Selling Real Estate and knows the WHY behind the WHY of what we do.

Any agent who is Certified in the Psychological Approach knows how to fit all the pieces of the puzzle together to create an award-winning strategy for your home.

Without the WHY and a larger set of core beliefs, you have a knock-off agent on your hands. You have someone who's offering you a Venti Frappuccino but can only make a cup of cold brew. They're just a cheap imitation.

Why not do business with the best?

Remember: Steve Jobs didn't just wake up one day and say that he was going to build the most profitable company in the world. He took baby steps. He studied human psychology; he hired the best team of engineers, and he became a master marketer. That is why we took to studying Steve Jobs and found out that these seven fundamental principles could be reverse-engineered and adapted to home selling.

The results have been amazing, and the stories and examples you have read in the book are testaments to that. We believe that the real estate industry needs to evolve and innovate to help buyers and sellers.

And if you are thinking of selling your home, you have three choices…

You could call the traditional real estate agent, the one with the "systems," the one who knows how to promote their business with stats about how many homes they have sold, or maybe they have a "Guaranteed-Sales-Program" with fine print.

Note: You will recognize this agent because they will come sit at your kitchen table and open their laptop with a "listing presentation," they will talk about "comps," and they will have their canned script. These "system" agents have a hard time innovating strategies themselves and are usually two or three years behind the curve.

Or, you could take what you have learned in this book and adapt the strategies yourself to help sell your home for maximum profit.

The strategies learned in this book are intended to increase the value, or the perceived value, of your home.

Why do people pay $700 for an iPhone that costs $249 to manufacture? Because there is a perceived valued to owning an iPhone. Potential buyers need to see the value in your home, and by following the seven strategies that I've outlined, you will increase the perceived value of your home.

Here's what you can do next...

If you have learned anything from this book, if just one of the fundamental strategies resonated with you and you had an "ah-ha" moment, then you understand the core beliefs we stand for.

If at any point, you've "raised your hand" in agreement, then our Approach will work well for you and your home.

Reach out to the certified agent who gave you this book. Give them a call.

Or, go to www.ClientProfitSecrets.com to learn more about the Approach. Click on "Contact" and a certified agent will reach out to you to setup a meeting.

We want to find out about you, your needs, your wants, your goals. You require a unique approach and strategy. What we might recommend for you, we might not recommend for your neighbor.

That's why within 48 hours of the initial meeting, you will have a full written report/game plan of the strategies that we are going to utilize for you. If you agree with those strategies, then we can work together. If not, then we shake hands, wish each other luck, and move in a different direction.

The small details matter.

Steve Jobs said it better than I ever could:

> When you're a carpenter making a beautiful chest of drawers, you're not going to use a piece of plywood on the back, even though it faces the wall and nobody will see it. You'll know it's there, so you're going to use a beautiful piece of wood on the back. For you to sleep well at night, the aesthetic, the quality, has to be carried all the way through.

Be diligent; choose wisely!

About The Author: In addition to showing homeowners how to sell their home for as much as $30,000 more than other similar homes on the market by treating their home as a "business" and by using the Seven Fundamental Strategies used by Steve Jobs to build Apple into the most profitable company in the world, Eric Verdi also authors and publishes a monthly newsletter, "The Eric Verdi Letter" – a sitcom-based newsletter with real life stories weaved into real estate. It also includes a segment called "Stories from the Street," where he weaves real life real estate transaction stories into a learning experience for readers.

Eric hosts a podcast, "Frederick Advice Givers," that gives local business owners and entrepreneurs a chance to share their story.

Eric is committed to the highest in customer satisfaction and giving each client individualized and specialized attention.

Eric is committed in giving back locally to many charities and events throughout the year, he is a committed and proud supporter of The Zachary Warfield Scholarship Fund (www.Zack5k.org), an annual scholarship given to deserving high school seniors both locally and in California, raising over $40,000 since 2013 for these amazing students.

In addition, Eric is co-founder of the powerful crowdfunding charity, Impact Club™, the Frederick Chapter is committed to infusing over $60,000 annually to local charities. To learn more and become a member of Impact Club Frederick™, go to www.ImpactClubFrederick.com

CHAPTER TWELVE

RECOMMENDED READING AND RESOURCES

Below is a list of books and resources that were read and either contributed to the thought process behind the theories or were directly used and quoted in this book.

Ariely, Dan "Predictably Irrational," *The Hidden Forces that Shape our Decisions*, 2008.

Beckwith, Harry "Selling the Invisible," *A Field Guide to Modern Marketing*, 1997.

Blumenthal, Karen "Steve Jobs, the Man Who Though Different," 2012.

Caples, John "Tested Advertising Methods," 5th Edition. 1997.

Cialdini, Robert B. (PH.D) "Influence," *The Psychology of Persuasion*, 2007.

Clason, George S. "The Richest Man In Babylon," 1988.

Ferriss, Timothy "The 4-Hour Workweek," *Escape 9-5, Live Anywhere, and Join the New Rich*, 2007.

RECOMMENDED READING AND RESOURCES

Gallo, Carmine "The Presentation Secrets of Steve Jobs," *How to be Insanely Great in Front of Any Audience*, 2010.

Gallo, Carmine "The Innovation Secrets of Steve Jobs," *Insanely Different Principles for Breakthrough Success*, 2011.

Gallo, Carmine "The Apple Experience," Secrets to Building Insanely Great Customer Loyalty, 2012.

Glenn, Joshua and Carol Hayes "Taking Things Seriously," *75 Objects with Unexpected Significance*, 2007.

Halbert, Gary C. "The Boron Letters," 2013.

Hardy, Darren "The Compound Effect," *Jumpstart Your Income, Your Life, Your Success*, 2010.

Hill, Napoleon "Think and Grow Rich," 2003.

Hill, Napoleon "The Law of Success," original 1925.

Issacson, Walter "Steve Jobs," 2011.

Kennedy, Dan "The Ultimate Sales Letter," 4th Edition. 2011.

Kennedy, Dan "No B.S. Guide to Brand Building by Direct Response," 2014.

Marshall, Perry "80/20 Sales and Marketing," *The Definitive Guide to Working Less and Making More*, 2013.

Michelli, Joseph A. "The Starbucks Experience," *5 Principles for Turning Ordinary into Extraordinary*, 2007.

Ogilvy, David "Ogilvy on Advertising," 1985.

Schwartz, Eugene M. "Breakthrough Advertising," 2004.

Sugarman, Joseph "Advertising Secrets of the Written Word," *The Ultimate Resource on How to Write Powerful Advertising Copy from One of America's Top Copywriters and Mail Order Entrepreneurs*, 1998.

Thiel, Peter "Zero to One," *Notes on Startups, or How to Build the Future*, 2014.

240-815-0890

www.ClientProfitSecrets.com

www.ingramcontent.com/pod-product-compliance
Lightning Source LLC
Chambersburg PA
CBHW051811170526
45167CB00005B/1964